STRIKE FROM SPACE

STRIKE

FROM SPACE

how the russians may destroy us

PHYLLIS SCHLAFLY
AND
CHESTER WARD
REAR ADMIRAL, UNITED STATES NAVY (RET.)

THE DEVIN-ADAIR COMPANY
NEW YORK 1966

The Soviet missile on the cover is a reproduction of the orbital rocket displayed in Moscow on Nov. 7, 1965 which *Tass* said could orbit the earth and be brought down on any target at the press of a button.

First hard cover edition, January 1966. A paperback edition of *Strike From Space* is available from the Pere Marquette Press, P.O. Box 316, Alton, Ill., at 75c.

PROLOGUE

The Secretary of State delivered a deeply emotional declaration on behalf of the United States:

"The threat of surprise attack . . . presents a constant danger. It is unacceptable that the Soviet political system should be given the opportunity to make secret preparations to face the free world with the choice of abject surrender or nuclear destruction."

The time was May 9, 1960; the Secretary was Christian Herter.

Five years later, space-age weapons have so intensified the Soviet threat that a group of non-Communist Americans is making secret preparations which will reduce the United States to exactly that choice. A "deal" — a surrender, if need be — is to their minds the only safe way out. Here is their ideology:

"Deal with the Devil we must, and come to some sort of terms with him we must. . . . If only for the reason that we are not *that* superior, for the reason that each of us, be it an individual or nation, has a little of the Devil in himself." — George F. Kennan.

This book is written for those Americans who instead believe that the two great guarantees of peace are the power of God and United States military strength; for people who affirm that belief in God is all that superior to atheism, that freedom is all that superior to slavery, that America is indeed all that superior to any Communist state, be it Soviet or Red Chinese; and that the future of America should be entrusted to the Power which has made and preserved us a nation, rather than to a deal with the Devil.

COMMENT BY AUTHORITIES

"*Strike from Space* is must reading for Americans who are profoundly concerned about our survival as a free people, in a free Republic, under the rule of God. The authors clearly define the awful dangers we face and the measures we must take to prevent nuclear annihilation. Those who love liberty and justice will act now! We are running out of time!"

Admiral Ben Moreell, USN (Ret.) World War II Chief of Civil Engineers, U.S. Navy. Organizer of the Navy's famed Seabees. Author of The Admiral's Log.

"This is a powerful book. The authors have skillfully assembled pertinent facts which have an urgent bearing on our security and our survival. They have made a convincing case against Communism and against those misguided Americans who refuse to recognize the seriousness of the threat that confronts us. It should be read by every American."

Brig. General William H. Wilbur, USA (Ret.) Recipient of the Congressional Medal of Honor. Author of Guideposts to the Future, *and* Freedom Must Not Perish.

"*Strike from Space* by Phyllis Schlafly and Rear Admiral Chester Ward, USN (Ret.) is an attempt to bring a very important message before the United States public, namely, that the road to world peace does not lie in the direction of disarmament, but rather in the maintenance of a posture of overwhelming strategic nuclear superiority. This has been our successful strategy for the last two decades. The vital question is: will we maintain this posture in the future, or will we go down the primrose path to disarmament and oblivion?"

General Thomas S. Power, USAF (Ret.) Commander in Chief of U.S. Strategic Air Command, 1957-1964. Author of Design for Survival.

TABLE OF CONTENTS

PART ONE

chapter I

THE WORLD'S GREATEST MYSTERY

Why did Lee Harvey Oswald kill President Kennedy? Why did Rudolf Hess, the No. 2 Nazi, fly solo to England in 1941, when Germany and England were at war? Why did John Wilkes Booth shoot President Lincoln after the Civil War had ended?

These are famous unsolved mysteries of history that still fascinate everyone. In the synthetic mysteries of fiction, the solutions can always be found — in earlier days by a Sherlock Holmes through an exercise of the mind; today by a James Bond or a Mickey Spillane, who, with little exercise of the mind but much of the body, can separate the good guys from the bad guys and, along the way, get all the girls, both good and bad.

Getting the girls and figuring out the solution in today's novels of sex and sadism are far easier than discovering the truth in a real-life mystery. There are other differences. One colossal contrast between the soft and sexy mysteries of fiction and the hard mysteries of reality is the size of their audiences. The James Bond, Mickey Spillane and Perry Mason books, movies and television programs have audiences in the millions.

Yet, what a knowledgeable newspaperman accurately called "the world's greatest mystery" passed its first birthday on October 14, 1965 — and not 195 Americans out of a nation of 195 million show any active interest in its solution. This real-life mystery, if not solved in time, will become the greatest tragedy in history. It will affect, in a life-or-death way, more millions of Americans than all the audiences of fiction mysteries combined.

It is no exaggeration of either mystery or potential tragedy to bill this as "the greatest." It is the first mystery to deal in *megadeaths* — a Pentagon term meaning "millions of deaths." At least 149 million Americans could be casualties of 3 of the 4 plans for world peace which motivate the characters of this mystery.

The figure of 149 megadeaths is not fiction. It is highly official — because it is the statement made by Secretary of Defense Robert Strange McNamara before the House Armed Services Committee in February 1965.[1] It is even more highly optimistic — because McNamara is *always* optimistic about such things. Remember his statement of October 2, 1964, which was issued through the White House in order to impress the public:

> "The major part of the United States military task [in Vietnam] can be completed by the end of 1965. . . . By the end of this year [1964] . . . the U.S. program should have progressed to the point where 1,000 U.S. military personnel can be withdrawn."[2]

Even the liberal press lists this now-famous Mc-Namara statement as No. 1 on his no-hit parade of major mistakes.

A more realistic estimate of potential American casualties resulting from the plots in this mystery would be 170 million — and those left living would envy the dead.

Yet our story *need not* end that way. The most important "first" presented by this greatest of mysteries is that *the readers themselves can change the ending.* The readers are the detectives, and they alone have the power to see that the good guys come out on top. This is because the best way to defeat a plot is to expose it. Once we correctly analyze the clues, the solution is easy.

When the Soviets sneaked their missiles into Cuba in 1962, the United States was saved from nuclear destruction by what U.S. Marine Corps General David M. Shoup called "the grace of God and an aerial photograph." The *knowledge* that the missiles were there was the major factor which enabled us to thwart the Cuba plot. Likewise, knowledge can enable us to thwart the new Kremlin plot for a *Space Cuba.*

The solution of "the world's greatest mystery" is itself the clue to the 3 plots described in this book. Each is separately motivated, but they interlock with prominent names and triplecross each other. All 3 can be foiled if the American people *know* what these men are planning for our future.

This book will enable the reader to penetrate many of the minor mysteries of "managed news." The basis of all military planning is to make an "estimate of the situation." To do this, we first need to learn much about the enemy and more about ourselves. Strengths and weaknesses, objectives, plans, and timetables must be compared. This book will assist the reader to make his own *estimate of the situation* so he can better understand enemies whose weapons range from sharpened bamboo poles to space-ships, from Pugwash brainwash to newspaper ads. This book will also help the reader to understand what a very few Americans are doing to America — and why they are doing it.

One reason for reading this real-life mystery — and thereby helping to change the ending — is that the prospective victims who can be saved are such nice people. In fiction mysteries, the victims are seldom attractive characters and never more than make-believe. In this stranger-than-fiction case, the potential victims are real people, good Americans: you, your family and your friends. The lives you save will be your own — and your loved ones!

chapter II

WHAT HAPPENED TO KHRUSHCHEV?

What is "the world's greatest mystery"? The syndicated columnist William S. White described it this way:

"The world's greatest mystery [is] the real meaning and implications for the West of the ouster of Nikita Khrushchev from power in the Soviet Union."[1]

General Dwight Eisenhower put his finger on the unique importance of this mystery when he said:

"There has to be some reason for throwing the man out. If we can determine the correct reason, then we would know how to cut our own cloth."[2]

Even *Newsweek* conceded:

"The much maligned art of Kremlinology has again become a matter of life and death."[3]

The new Soviet bosses, Brezhnev and Kosygin, released a 40-page explanation of why Nikita had to go, which accused Khrushchev of 29 sins including:

"He tried to make wife Nina chairman of the Union of Soviet Women, he 'antagonized intellectuals,' and clung to uneconomical building plans (he insisted on 5-story rather than 12-story apartment houses, on underpasses rather than overpasses)."[4]

Such trivia were obviously false clues planted to divert attention from the truth. According to *Time*, "Khrushchev's gravest error" among the 29 sins was that he "let Mao Tse-tung gain valuable prestige by exploding his bomb without warning."[5] Actually, there is no evidence that Red China tried to keep her bomb a secret! Even the U.S. State Department knew about Red China's first nuclear explosion many months in advance — and kept our Asian allies fully informed. It could not possibly have surprised the Soviets, who had furnished the initial know-how, industrial equipment, and even basic explosive materials for the Chinese nuclear program.

The liberal consensus in the United States was that Khrushchev was ousted because he used poor judgment in "unduly exacerbating the Sino-Soviet split." But Brezhnev's policy toward Red China is just as tough as Khrushchev's. Suslov, one of the leaders of the ousting, is far more deeply hated by the Chinese Reds than Khrushchev. He was the chief articulate instrument of Khrushchev's war of words with the Red Chinese.

By far the most exciting clue in the Khrushchev mystery was hidden in another major charge advanced in the Kremlin document:

"Khrushchev did not consult the all-powerful Party Presidium when he made the 'serious' mistake of sending missiles to Cuba."[6]

This charge is absurd. Execution of the plan took more than a year, cost more than a billion dollars. The problems of transportation, engineering, construction, communications, defense, electronics, personnel, and security were so complex that it must have been an all hands, top-priority effort for the Soviet leadership.

There is far more dramatic proof that this Kremlin assertion is a big Communist lie designed to fool the American people. During the entire preparation of the plot to sneak missiles into Cuba, there were two other members of the Soviet Presidium who attended all the top-secret planning conferences with Khrushchev and Castro. Who were Khrushchev's two highest-level co-conspirators?

Cuban Co-Conspirators

The two chief co-conspirators who plotted with Khrushchev and Castro to put Soviet nuclear power close enough to destroy the United States were *Leonid I. Brezhnev and Aleksei N. Kosygin.*

In other words, *the two men who replaced Khrushchev were the same two men who were Khrushchev's co-conspirators when he sent Soviet missiles into Cuba!* Why has this vital information been hidden from the American people? Obviously, so that "managed news" could present Brezhnev and Kosygin as "peace-loving Communists in gray flannel suits."

The CIA and the State Department must have known this all along. Read what was written on May 15, 1963, in the column of Joseph Alsop, close and loyal friend of the then President John Kennedy:

"The Soviet Defense Minister, Marshal Rodion Malinovsky, who is not a Presidium member, nonetheless attended all the Soviet leaders' meetings with Fidel Castro, even though *the most important meetings were otherwise restricted to Nikita S. Khrushchev and two other Presidium members, Leonid I. Brezhnev and Aleksei N. Kosygin.*"[7] (emphasis added)

When Alsop wrote this, the names Brezhnev and Kosygin were almost unknown to the American public. At that time no one could have foreseen the ouster of Khrushchev; the meetings referred to were held in the spring and summer of 1962. Yet, after Khrushchev was removed, this startling fact was never again discussed in our press.

In order to determine the correct reason for Khrushchev's ouster, so "we would know how to cut our own cloth," "all the elaborate machinery of the tremendous U.S. spook industry was swiftly and silently put to work."[8] Yet, President Johnson admitted he did not know the answer.[9]

After the event, CIA and State Department Kremlinologists came up with a "solution" so absurd that it could only have been invented in Foggy Bottom. They said that Khrushchev was deposed because he had advocated spending more capital on agriculture and consumer goods.[10] Yet the new Premier picked to replace Khrushchev, Aleksei Kosygin, was Khrushchev's own Gosplan director, who had been running the economic system for Khrushchev. Furthermore, if the CIA-State "solution" were true, the economic "New Deal" announced by Kosygin September 27, 1965 would have abandoned Khrushchev policies — but instead it extends the "profit" type incentives and other key Khrushchev innovations.

In the days following the sensational ouster of Khrushchev, all the news media jumped into the game of playing amateur detective. Their leads led down blind alleys because liberals interpret all Soviet actions in the light (or the fog) of their own false preconceptions. Thus *Newsweek* asserted that "Russia today [is] still . . . a riddle wrapped in a mystery inside an enigma," and predicted that "the full story of Khrushchev's disgrace may not become known for months, or years . . . or perhaps forever." *Time* concluded that we must peer "into the weird logic and dark motivations of Communism."[11]

Khrushchev's "Own Boys"

Thus, the simple solution became invisible to the experts, and they missed the clues in their own reports. Hidden in *Time's* own account was this significant clue:

"Both Brezhnev and Kosygin were hand-picked by Nikita to buttress his domain, and consequently in the past they had represented many of his own ideas and methods. On the face of it, they now stand for '*Khrushchevism without Khrushchev*' — the same show run more smartly, more carefully."[12]

Time showed that Khrushchev's overthrow was not accomplished by a new crowd, but by Khrushchev's "own boys." *The New York Times,* in a comprehensive feature on the "why of Khrushchev's ouster," included another important point:

"In the power shift, it was stressed, the role of the Soviet military was vital if not conclusive."[13]

Khrushchev's ouster was supported by the

rabidly anti-U.S. Chief of the Soviet Armed Forces, Marshal Malinovsky.[14] A UPI Dispatch added a third clue: that Brezhnev praised "the Soviet Party leadership's *unanimous* vote to unseat Khrushchev."[15]

Thus, Khrushchev must have been overthrown because of something so vital to both civilians and military that it unanimously turned against him "his own boys," the leaders of the Soviet armed forces, and all the Communist Party officials. What could be of such importance that it could bring about the downfall of the most "popular" and successful dictator Communism ever produced? Let us examine the men who ousted Khrushchev.

Foremost was President of the Soviet Union, Leonid Brezhnev, who had been selected by Khrushchev himself as heir-apparent. Brezhnev was czar of the Soviet space and rocket programs, and in 1961 was declared "Hero of the Soviet Union" for his outstanding services in the space program. Brezhnev was also Chairman of the Military Affairs Committee of the Communist Party and a Lieutenant General in the Soviet Army. He and Khrushchev were the only high-ranking Party leaders to hold military rank also.

The second man involved in the Khrushchev ouster was Mikhail Suslov — also a close associate and protege of Khrushchev. Suslov is Chairman of the Foreign Policy Commission of the Communist Party. He was one of those who helped Khrushchev put down the threatened coup in 1956-7. As the recognized Party theoretician, Suslov presented the public version of the purported "charges" against Khrushchev, including nepotism, fostering a personality cult, one-man rule, errors of policy, and harebrained scheming.

The third man in the triumvirate that overthrew Khrushchev was Nikolai V. Podgorny, Chairman of the Internal Security Affairs Commission of the Communist Party. He also is a longtime close associate of Khrushchev.

Summing up the factors common to the three leaders of the Khrushchev ouster, each is chairman of a key committee of the Communist Party, and each is vitally concerned with Soviet military and weapons programs, and plans for world conquest. All three were close personal associates of Khrushchev, and two of the three had in the past risked their careers and even their lives to back Khrushchev in a political crisis. Add to the list Kosygin, who took over Khrushchev's No. 2 job as Premier of the Soviet Union, and the clique includes both of Khrushchev's Presidium-level co-conspirators in the Cuban missile plot.

In order to interpret the meaning of these facts, let us imagine a parallel situation in the United States. Suppose the Chairman of the Joint Chiefs of Staff, the Secretaries of State and Defense, the Directors of the FBI and CIA, and the Chairmen of the Senate and House Armed Services Committee, all joined together in forcing the resignation of a President who had been in office for a number of years and was obviously popular with the people and his party. Suppose further that the men who demanded his resignation had a consistent record of personal loyalty to the President and had in the past even risked their own careers to advance his. Suppose that the proceedings to force the resignation were conducted in secret. Finally, suppose that the President, who had heretofore been the most powerful man in the country, resigned, and thereafter lived in retirement enjoying the comforts of a man of means and influence.

Under these circumstances, it would not be too difficult to deduce that the hypothetical President (1) had tremendously and unnecessarily — but not willfully — endangered U.S. national security, and (2) had resigned in order to repair the damage and as his contribution to the fulfillment of objectives he had worked for as President.

Can it be that the ousting of Khrushchev was really in the nature of an impeachment for carelessness rather than criminality — a *forced resignation* cunningly contrived by the Soviets to look to the world like the usual power grab, but actually to cover up the damage Khrushchev had done to their secret war plan? Let us take a close look at the real Khrushchev, certainly the most vivid, volatile and vituperative personality ever to spout the Marxist dialectic.

Khrushchev's "Shoot the Sheriff" Plan

All true Communists, of whom Khrushchev certainly is one, are dedicated to the Communist conquest of the world as the essential pre-condition to their other principal objectives, such as permanent world "peace" and the Communist organization of all industrial and agricultural production on a worldwide basis.[16] Khrushchev not only believes in the Communist conquest of the world, but also that it is his historic mission to bring about this conquest:

"In the short time I have to live, I would like to see the day when the Communist flag flies over the whole world."[17]

Khrushchev had become very contemptuous of U.S. leadership and cocksure that his dream would come true. He delighted in making offhand graphic statements of his goals, often wrapped in an insult to the United States, such as: "I spit in their faces and they call it dew."

In late 1960, the 81 Communist Parties of the world attended a conference in Moscow and adopted a new *Manifesto* updating their strategy for world conquest which would be pursued until "final victory" at a "time no longer far off." On January 6, 1961 Khrushchev interpreted this *Moscow Manifesto* in a long speech which the AP Moscow Bureau called the most important Soviet pronouncement since the end of World War II.

The speech was immediately recognized by the press and the politicians, as a Communist blueprint for world conquest. Even the *Washington Post* and *The Reporter* deplored it. Secretary of State Rusk cited it, and President Kennedy assigned it as required reading by all top officials on military and foreign policy.[18]

Only the most objective experts, however, faced the full implications of terror in the Khrushchev speech. The American Security Council *Washington Report* analyzed it as containing "plans to eliminate the United States as 'the enemy of the peoples of the world', by preventive war."[19] The most comprehensive evaluation was made by Dr. Stefan T. Possony, Director of the Hoover Institute at Stanford University, and published by the Government Printing Office. Extensively documented, brilliantly developed, and logically irrefutable, his 100-page analysis is the most authentic expose of the secret Soviet war plan, a plan which

> ". . . utilizes massive deception to bring about, through (a) the unilateral weakening of the free world, (b) the moral paralysis of free world governments, and (c) the demoralization of public opinion, the capitulation of the United States. Failing in this strategy, the Soviet intends to destroy the United States by nuclear weapons."[20]

This Khrushchev speech revealed the broad plan by which the Soviet Union intends "to destroy the United States by nuclear weapons," without itself being subjected to fatal, or even seriously crippling, damage from U.S. retaliation. Khrushchev had become convinced that the Soviets could not complete their conquest of the world without having at some point to face nuclear resistance from the United States; therefore, the only way to avert enormous damage to the Soviet Union is to surprise us and wipe us out.

Most important, Khrushchev had discovered the basic fact of the nuclear age: U.S. *weapons* are protected against surprise attack by burying them in concrete silos or submerging them under the oceans — but our people are *not* protected. Khrushchev's logic was as clear as his conclusion was amoral: he decided the *population* of the United States would be the *No. 1 military target of nuclear weapons!* Before Khrushchev's speech, nuclear strategy had targeted masses of people only for terror, blackmail or demoralization.

Khrushchev is very practical — not sophisticated like McNamara's "Whiz Kids." He discovered a practical solution. Americans can understand it as the "Shoot the Sheriff" plan. When wild western outlaws planned to ambush the sheriff, they did not rely on shooting the guns out of his holsters to prevent him from shooting back. They would *shoot the sheriff*. The guns might be invulnerable, but he was not.

Americans are inclined to disbelieve this threat because it is too shocking. All the evidence we have of Soviet technological advances, however, indicates they are racing ahead in strategic nuclear weapons and space weapons of the type useful for the Khrushchev strategy. The entire Soviet strategic weapons program, scientific, technological, productional and operational, can be explained only as especially designed for a massive surprise attack. It is far more precisely designed for carrying out the assassination of a whole people than Oswald's mail-order rifle, fitted with telescopic sights, was suited for the assassination of one special person.

Khrushchev's sending his offensive missiles into Cuba in 1962 was a daring attempt to accelerate the timing of his surprise strike. He took the risk that the U.S. might prematurely discover the missiles and strike to disarm the Soviets. On the other hand, if Khrushchev's strategy had succeeded, he could have utterly destroyed the power and people of the United States. When the U-2 photographs deprived him of the element of surprise, he had to fall back on his original plan of a strike from space — the preparations for which our U-2 planes cannot photograph.

The following year, other clues began to reveal the Kremlin strategy. In July 1963, British astronomer Sir Bernard Lovell returned from a visit to the Soviet Union with a report that the Soviets saw nothing of value in sending a man to the moon.[21] Also that year, Khrushchev told reporters:

> "We are not at present planning flights by cosmonauts to the moon. . . . I have a report to the effect that the Americans want to land a man on the moon by 1970-80. Well, let's wish them success. . . . We shall take their experience into account. We do not want to compete with the sending of people to the moon without careful preparation."

Newsweek commented on this quote:

> "Khrushchev may have been out to trick the Americans, but it is more likely that the statement was true. In fact, Khrushchev's frankness may have contributed to his downfall."[22]

If the Soviets are not running a space race to the moon, then the huge space effort, into which the Soviets have put $20 billion in the last 5 years, must have a *military* purpose.

The next major clue to the Kremlin's master plan appeared a year later. On August 15, 1964, Khrushchev granted a 3-hour interview to Lord

Thompson, a Canadian-born English newspaper magnate. Lord Thompson asked Khrushchev if he favored a summit conference aimed at banning nuclear weapons. Khrushchev replied, "We would be ready," but expressed doubt that such an agreement would be effective because:

> "The trouble is that the losing side will always use nuclear weapons in the last resort to avoid defeat. If a man thinks he is going to die, he'll take any steps."[23]

In this one sentence, Khrushchev let slip the fact that the Soviets must have a "preventive strategy," that is, a plan for a surprise attack on the United States. Communists are very logical and, once they came to the conclusion that nuclear war is inevitable, then it is obviously better to deliver the first blow. In this one sentence Khrushchev clarified many previous statements, such as:

> "A fight is in progress between these two systems, a life and death combat. But we Communists want to win this struggle with the least losses and there is no doubt whatsoever that we shall win."[24]

Once the Soviets decided that the "losing side" (which by definition must be the United States, since the Soviets think they are "sure to win") would inevitably use nuclear weapons to defend itself, the only way the Soviets can *surely win* "with the *least losses*" is by a surprise first strike.

The Khrushchev interview with Lord Thompson was reported by the Associated Press and carried by practically every member paper — because the same interview also included a statement by Khrushchev about Barry Goldwater, who was front-page news at the time. Significantly, no direct report of this 3-hour interview was ever published in Russia.

The "Monstrous New Terrible Weapon"

On September 15, 1964, Khrushchev received a group of visiting Japanese trade representatives and journalists and made his third slip. Headlines around the world screamed out Khrushchev's announcement that the Soviets had a "monstrous new terrible weapon" — a weapon capable of wiping out life on earth. Speculation ranged worldwide; U.S. television and radio featured it; scholars deduced that he was referring to an orbital bomb or to multiple warheads for missiles;[25] millions of Americans began to worry about it. What did the Soviets plan to do with this monstrous weapon? Why had they spent huge resources to develop it?

Then a strange thing happened. Two days later Khrushchev recanted. At first, in obvious confusion, he said an explanation would be issued next Tuesday. Almost immediately, however, he went further and declared he had been misquoted. *Time* observed:

> "It was quite a performance, and one that only a dictator could bring off."[26]

Why had Khrushchev said what he did? Nothing at all was to be gained by his statement that the use of nuclear weapons was "inevitable." Very little was to be gained by his claim of the "monstrous new terrible weapon," unless perhaps he was trying to help out Lyndon Johnson's campaign of nuclear terror which had been inaugurated one week earlier in his Labor Day speech at Detroit.

The most probable reason for Khrushchev's slip that nuclear war was "inevitable" is that he thinks about the Soviet plan for preventive war all the time, and it just popped out. Just as obscene books are a good clue to the thoughts and private lives of their authors, so Khrushchev's frequent remarks about nuclear terror are a reliable clue to Soviet strategy. Khrushchev's typical greeting to Western diplomats was:

> "You know, they say that in order to destroy your country all one needs is 6 H-bombs, perhaps 9 at the most. I have 12, all set aside just for you."[27]

The only other apparent reason for Khrushchev's bad judgment, for the unnecessary risks he took with secret Soviet plans, was overconfidence. In his breezy way, as teenagers would say, "he shot off his big mouth." Having duped us into the nuclear test ban, and then duped us again by his promise not to send offensive missiles into Cuba, he was supremely overconfident of his own power to say whatever he wanted. The chances are that, if he had said:

> We have developed a monstrous new terrible weapon in order to launch a surprise attack against the United States so massive that retaliation will be practically impossible,

American liberals would respond:

Khrushchev doesn't really mean to threaten us — he is just trying to scare the Chinese Communists, and if we give him a few chemical plants and machine tools, this will widen the rift.

To the more conservative Soviet leaders, however, Khrushchev's slips had created tremendous risks. He had jeopardized their plan for world conquest, plus the Soviet investment of years of time and hundreds of billions of dollars wrung out of a poor economy. With 3 slips of the tongue, Khrushchev had revealed the Soviet plan for a surprise strike from space — priceless knowledge the CIA and other U.S. intelligence agents could not otherwise have discovered until too late.

The Soviets simply could not afford to take a chance that these two interviews in 1964, which received wide coverage in the U.S. press, would be taken seriously, because, as Eisenhower said, then the U.S. "would know how to cut its own cloth." They knew this would mean *an entry* by the U.S. in the race for military control of the world through space weapons, plus *a re-entry* by the U.S. in the strategic arms race in bombers, super-missiles and anti-missiles. The Soviets know that, if America really goes all out, it would bankrupt the Soviets to compete. As of the time they began to show alarm in the Kremlin, their intelligence could have easily discovered that Khrushchev's strategy of surprise attack had been clearly described in a scholarly article in an important U.S. strategic publication[28] and, in laymen's language, in a paperback book which sold 2,000,000 copies.[29] The Soviets also knew they had the

Voskhod space spectacular on the way in less than a month, which would further awaken Americans about Soviet missiles and space ships.

The task of the Soviet leadership was, first, to insure that Khrushchev would have no more chances to talk too much about secret war plans. But, if this were all, he could have been retired with all the window dressing of a legitimate transfer of power, with great propaganda advantages. The more important part of their task was to provide "cover" to prevent U.S. leadership from taking Khrushchev's warnings seriously. The entire act had to appear to have nothing to do with Soviet war plans. It was necessary to oust Khrushchev in such a way that it would appear that Khrushchev's strategy was his alone — one of his harebrained schemes — and that Brezhnev and Kosygin disavowed such warlike plans. So they surrounded the ousting with all the trappings of a traditional coup common to dictatorships.

All the evidence indicates that Khrushchev was, in effect, *forced to resign* because he had uselessly and almost fatally risked secret Soviet plans which depend on secrecy for their success. Only this explains the relationship of the leaders of the so-called "coup" to Soviet war plans, to Soviet security, and the fact that they were all close associates of Khrushchev. No other explanation tallies with Khrushchev's reversing himself publicly about the "monstrous new terrible weapon." If Japanese Premier Tojo had made a slip of the tongue in 1941 partially revealing his Pearl Harbor plans, he certainly would have been forced to resign!

Since the ouster, all subsequent events confirm this conclusion. At first, Khrushchev was treated to just the right amount of "disgrace" to pretend that his ousting was an ordinary coup. As the months rolled by without the Johnson-Humphrey Administration taking notice of Khrushchev's 3 slips, it became clear to the new Kremlin leaders that Khrushchev was right in believing that Americans would ignore even the clearest warnings.

So Khrushchev is being eased out of "disgrace" by subtle stages. In March 1965, Mrs. Khrushchev was permitted to appear at the opera. After this feeler produced no shocks, Khrushchev himself was allowed to make a public appearance.[30]

When the facts finally emerged, it became clear that Khrushchev was right in believing that Ameri-done anything malevolent against the Soviet Union. From the first he had a country home, a limousine and chauffeur. In February, 1965 he was given a luxurious 5-room apartment at 19 Staro-Koniusheny, next door to the Canadian Embassy— only a block from the Kremlin. Not only has he attended elections and art exhibits — but he has been seen going in and out of the Kremlin.[31] Is it more likely that his visits to the Kremlin offices are for friendly chats over old times with his former friends who ousted him — or for consultations on the secret Kremlin strategy for world conquest?

The way is thus prepared for Khrushchev to go down in history as the greatest Communist of all time — the one who planned and almost completed the strategy for world conquest, but who in the final stage resigned in order to make sure that his plan was carried through with the surprise which would guarantee its success — an act which would provide the object - lesson required to enforce worldwide discipline for the Communist cause.

Meanwhile the liberal press and the Administration have built up a mythical image of the new Kremlin bosses as "Communists in gray flannel," as "managers" rather than military men. They ignore Brezhnev's 25 years of military service. They ignore the fact that Brezhnev and Kosygin were co-conspirators in the Cuban missile plot. They ignore the fact that the vitriolic words of the new Kremlin leaders are exceeded only by their hostile actions in Vietnam.

Just as it often takes a thief to catch a thief, a Communist can often best understand another Communist's true character. A UPI Dispatch from Moscow dated June 21, 1965, said:

> "To the Chinese, Premier Aleksei N. Kosygin, and Party Chief Leonid I. Brezhnev are more formidable adversaries than Khrushchev had been. 'They are more subtle and more cunning and therefore more dangerous,' the Chinese have said."

Five months later, the Chinese Communists added this colorful postscript to their description of the new Kremlin masters:

> "The Chinese Communist 'People's Daily' said Khrushchev's successors are 'much more cunning and demoniac than he was.'"[32]

chapter III

MAKE A NOISE IN VIETNAM

The 15 Decisive Battles of the World is a favorite book of military historians. Some day, when the book is brought up to date, it should include the naval battle that took place on August 2 and 4, 1964 in the Bay of Tonkin. When the Monitor and the Merrimack are forgotten, the Battle of Tonkin Bay may still shape world history.

On August 2 and 4, 1964, several Communist motor torpedo boats attacked the most powerful fleet in the world, the U.S. Seventh Fleet. Why?

They could not have expected to inflict any major damage. These little torpedo boats pitted themselves against the most advanced shipboard radar in the world. They were fantastically outnumbered and out-gunned. With no air cover of their own, the torpedo boats put themselves within range of the Seventh Fleet's many modern fighter and attack aircraft. What could these torpedo boats expect other than to make a puny appearance — and then get sunk or chased home? That is exactly what happened.

For a few days, newspapers and magazines in the United States, television and radio commentators, all repeated the question: *Why?* It was another real-life mystery, stranger than fiction could

28

conceive. When the answer did not come as rapidly as readers of James Bond and Perry Mason expected, the American public moved on to other interests.

Thus it was not realized that the Communist motor torpedo boats had accomplished their mission with a resounding success. What was that mission?

Up until August 2-4, 1964, American military personnel were in the Vietnamese area as advisers only. But on August 5, 1964, as a result of these futile attacks,

> "direct attacks were made by U.S. carrier-based aircraft on North Vietnam, the first such action of this war. . . . At the same time the U.S. began a large-scale deployment of forces to the areas of Southeast Asia. . . . On August 7, Congress went on record by an overwhelming vote in support of the tough new stand."[1]

In other words, as a result of a deliberate provocation, carefully planned and exquisitely timed, the United States began the long fall into the trap of a shooting war not only with the Viet Cong, but also with the regular forces of Ho Chi Minh.

The persistence of the Communist planners in attaining this result is significant. The first attack was made on the U.S.S. Maddox on August 2. In times past, nations had gone to war on less provocation. But the only reaction from the U.S. was self-defensive firing at the Communist boats. So the Communists tried again two days later. They knew that America was on the eve of a presidential election campaign. The incumbent Administration was basing its campaign largely on its promise to maintain peace through strength. It had issued torrents of statistics claiming military superiority, particularly in *conventional* weapons. Some response had to be made, or the Administration would go into the campaign branded as "soft" on Communism and weak in the face of Red military strength. President Lyndon Johnson ordered the retaliation against North Vietnam, and the Communist torpedo boats thereby accomplished their mission.

The attacks against the Seventh Fleet were the first in a long string of carefully-plotted provocations, including the attack on the American Embassy and the Pleiku U.S. barracks, the bombing of the U.S. officers' billet in Saigon, the death by torture of American prisoners of war, the public execution of U.S. soldiers, and the attempt to assassinate Ambassador Maxwell Taylor just before his departure from Saigon in July 1965.

These actions had little military value. They were recognized in official White House statements as "direct provocations by the Hanoi regime."[2] Their effect was to trap the United States into a shooting war *with conventional weapons* against minor targets in Vietnam.

Why do the Communists want the United States fighting in Vietnam? Why did they deliberately provoke us into bombing North Vietnam? *Surprise,* through diverting the attention of the enemy, has been the aggressor's winning stratagem since history began. The classic expression of this doctrine of diversion is attributed by some to the ancient Chinese strategist, Sun-Tzu, more than 2,000 years ago; others cite a perhaps legendary military expert, Tu-Yu, 1,000 years ago. It has been handed down to us compressed into 11 words:

"Make a noise in the East, but strike in the West."

This age-old stratagem still works in the nuclear-space age, and the Kremlin strategists are working it to death — our death, that is. In 1948-49 the Communists made a noise in Berlin and posted the Berlin Blockade. While we strained for 17 months to fly food and coal into Berlin, the Reds captured China. In 1958 they made a noise like binding themselves to a nuclear test ban. This so successfully diverted U.S. attention from the race for nuclear supremacy that we stopped running. After 3 years of secret preparations, they launched their surprise "strike" — in the form of massive ban-breaking tests which seized from the U.S. our former 2-to-1 lead in the technology of high-yield nuclear warheads — the only weapons powerful enough to control the world.

In 1962 the Soviets again made a "noise in the East" — by demanding immediate settlement of the Berlin problem under threat of a separate peace treaty with East Germany. This successfully diverted attention from the massive preparations they were making to "strike in the West" by sneaking their offensive missiles into Cuba. Again this classic stratagem worked, and the U.S. was caught off-guard.

The Battle of Tonkin Bay in 1964 launched the new version of "make a noise in the East, but strike in the West." In technology and in violence, in deaths and in damage, one end of the spectrum of warfare is an attack using space ships to deliver "gigaton" warheads (warheads in the thousand-megaton range; that is, with the explosive power of more than a thousand million tons of TNT). What is as far removed from that, as East is from West? The answer is, of course, *guerrilla war*. And next furthest removed is limited *conventional war*.

Vietnam is as far to the East of Washington as is geographically possible. American boys are bogged down in that little country, 12 hours of suntime and half-a-world away. One of the chief weapons against which our soldiers must defend themselves is the sharpened bamboo pole — more primitive even than the bow and arrow. While the enemy is waging a guerrilla war, our men are fighting a "conventional" war. The bombs we use are not even as powerful as we used in World War II. We have turned back the clock to World War I and measure our explosive power in *pounds* of TNT.

The guerrilla-conventional war in Vietnam is brilliantly successful in diverting U.S. attention from Soviet capabilities in space. All our present efforts are concentrated on expanding our conventional war capabilities. Billions are being spent to provide equipment and weapons for Vietnam. Production lines long since abandoned for mass manufacture of old-style ammunition and propeller airplanes are reactivated. Draft calls are increased; thousands of American foot soldiers and Marines are shipped out for jungle combat.

Every billion spent on old-style weapons, ships, aircraft, and the men to use them, means a billion dollars less for research, development and production of advanced weapons capable of deterring a Soviet surprise attack launched against us with nuclear space weapons. Our involvement in Vietnam not only diverts money, but it also diverts public and even Congressional attention from our defense against a space age Pearl Harbor.

Obvious vs. Hidden Dangers

Soviet plans are typically characterized by sensational boldness, brilliant simplicity, and chilling ruthlessness. Soviet strategists *never* permit their *major* plan to become obvious to Americans. One of the effective Communist techniques is to confront the United States simultaneously with other and *obvious* dangers less lethal or immediate than the one involved in the principal plan. The idea is to capture the attention of the U.S. leadership and public by persuading them to focus on the lesser danger.

Thus, during the first nuclear test ban, the obvious danger was Soviet cheating in the sub-kiloton and kiloton range through secret underground nuclear tests. The simple and bold plan instead was to make lengthy preparations for surprise atmospheric testing in the multi-megaton range.

During the Cuban crisis, the obvious danger was the buildup of conventional weapons to make the island a base for Communist subversion throughout Latin America. The actual plan — bold, simple and ruthless — was secretly to send to Cuba at least 42 2,200-mile range nuclear missiles capable of incinerating targets in 2/3 of the United States.

In the dispute about Vietnam, the "doves" are warning about the terrible danger of "escalation."[3] The "hawks" are warning that surrender in Vietnam will start the falling dominoes in Asia and enable the Communists to complete their conquest of the world on the installment plan. These two dangers have one characteristic in common: they are both very *obvious;* they are easy to believe. That fact alone should warn us that *neither* of these two dangers is really the most massive threat posed by the "masters of deceit." These obvious dangers must be a "cover" for a "third threat" — the threat from space. Nuclear warheads, delivered by orbital missiles, are the threat *least resembling,* and hence *best disguised by* — the two *obvious* dangers in Vietnam.

Soviet plans usually involve violation of a solemn Soviet promise. Thus, Khrushchev assured President Eisenhower that Russia would *not* test nuclear weapons as long as we didn't test. Gromyko assured President Kennedy in October 1962 that Russia had *not* placed offensive weapons in Cuba.

Ancient Troy's famous warning against the wooden horse treachery, "Fear the Greeks bearing gifts," should be updated to: "Fear the Communists when they make promises." All Communists practice what Stalin preached:

"Words must have no relation to action — otherwise what kind of diplomacy is it? . . . Good words are a mask for concealment of bad deeds. Sincere diplomacy is no more possible than dry water or iron wood."[4]

The outstanding agreement now in effect is the U.S.-U.S.S.R. adherence to the UN prohibition against orbital weapons in space. Another reason for being suspicious of it is that it was engineered in Yugoslavia at the 11th Pugwash Conference in September 1963.[5]

The $1 Billion Question

The Soviets are calling the shots in Vietnam. It was Kosygin (not Mao Tse-tung) who visited Hanoi in 1965 and urged the "liberation" of South Vietnam. Brezhnev and Kosygin have sent to North Vietnam large quantities of military supplies, including the most advanced SAM (surface-to-air) missiles, manned by Russians, to shoot down American flyers. The war materiel for the Viet Cong comes from Black Sea freighters, not Chinese junks. On August 25, 1965 the truce terms demanded by the North Vietnamese were issued in *Russian* by the North Vietnamese Embassy *in Moscow*.[6]

The proof that the Soviets really want the United States fighting in Vietnam is their long refusal to accept repeated American offers to negotiate. History shows that the Communists have a perfect record of besting the West at every conference table, from Teheran in 1943 (the minutes of which our State Department is too ashamed to make public) to the 1963 Moscow Test Ban Treaty.

The Reds know from the negotiations in China in 1946, in Geneva in 1954 concerning Vietnam, and over Laos in 1962, that they *always* leave the conference table controlling more real estate and people than when they arrived. They also know that President Johnson has been under tremendous pressure from leading members of his own party, such as Senators Fulbright, Mansfield, Gruening, Morse, and Church, to make large concessions for a face-saving pullout of Vietnam. Why would the Reds refuse to follow their usual tactic of winning more at the conference table than they could ever obtain on the battlefield?

How could the Communists reject President Johnson's tempting offer to give $1 billion to Mekong Valley and even let the Communists help dole out our money — when all they had to do to cash in on this handout was agree to "unlimited discussions"? This is the $1 billion question. U.S. "trial balloons" have signalled the Communists time and time again that the Administration is "unconditionally ready" to pull out on the basis of any face-saving negotiated settlement.[7] The Communists could take over all Vietnam within a year or two if we merely accepted the same arrangement the Kennedy-Johnson Administration agreed to in Laos. It is possible that the bait offered to the Communists by the State Department will be so tempting that they will decide "a bird in the hand is worth more than two in the bush." Since the aggressor calls the shots, the Reds could then make a noise anywhere else in the East to cover their plans to strike in the West.

The reason the Soviets refused for so many long months to let the U.S. pull out of Vietnam even at the price of a concealed surrender is that the Soviets are not trying to win *just* Vietnam — they plan to conquer the entire world. This they cannot do unless they first destroy the strategic nuclear power of the United States. Our *conventional* military power, such as we used in Korea and are now using in Vietnam, is *not* an effective obstacle to Communist world conquest. Our civilian and military leaders both repeatedly say that our available *conventional* strength is not enough to *win* the war against North Vietnam — and Vietnam is not a 2nd-rate power, not a 3rd-rate power, but a 30th-rate power! Comparing our conventional strength to the Soviets, we have 16 divisions, and they have 170 — plus more than twice as much modern conventional military equipment and weapons. Their divisions are not so large as ours, nor are they all at full strength; but their reserves outnumber ours by at least 3 to 1, and they can mobilize rapidly.

Small wonder, therefore, that the Soviets want to divert us into spending our military billions on conventional tactical equipment and training more foot soldiers. They are so far ahead in this field that we could never win in any local area on their side of the world — and *even if we could,* it would not deter them from winning the world by nuclear **means.**

Thus, the Soviets have made a revolutionary improvement on the old strategem of "Make a noise in the East, and strike in the West." It used to be that the "noise" was merely a feint, a ruse, a false alarm. But now, by holding us in a conventional war in Vietnam, the Soviets are forcing us to divert not merely our attention, but our men and our money away from the main threat, which is the nuclear threat. The Soviets know we simply can't afford to lose in Vietnam. A surrender or a defeat, even if covered by a face-saving formula, will indeed start the fall of the dominoes in Asia.

Vietnam is thus the newest and most deadly diversion ever devised by a cunning and ruthless aggressor. Before examining the clues which lead to the big strike in the West, let us look at the other devices by which the Soviets conceal their real plans from Americans.

chapter IV

THE CHAMPION CONFIDENCE GAME

Even though they have diverted us in Vietnam, how can the Communists, who are very practical people, reasonably expect to keep hidden from Americans a surprise strike in the West of any magnitude? Any kind of strike, in the nuclear age, requires months of preparation and great quantities of long lead-time equipment. Is the Soviet plan just a Red fairy tale like the phony promise of the "withering away of the state"?

The Communists can point with pride to their success as confidence men *par excellence:* smooth, fast talking, persuading us to risk our inheritance of freedom and independence for the false promises they dangle under our noses.

Stalin was the original Red confidence man; he started as a bank robber. What Stalin wanted was as plain as the moustache on his face. But he pulled the wool over President Roosevelt's eyes so that, just before Teheran, F.D.R. made this revealing statement:

> "I have just a hunch that Stalin doesn't want anything but security for his country, and I think that if I give him everything I possibly can and ask nothing from him in return, noblesse oblige, he won't try to annex anything and will work for a world democracy and peace."[1]

Roosevelt followed his hunch at Teheran and Yalta, and Stalin fleeced him of Eastern Europe, control of China, and three votes in the UN.

Fidel Castro was another successful confidence man. He fooled all the liberals. The *New York Times* told us that Castro was the Abraham Lincoln of Cuba. Well, he is tall, he is a lawyer, and he has a black beard — but no reasonable person can find any other similarity to Lincoln. After Castro was in power and sent his enemies "to the wall," he made quite a speech in which he laughed at us. He said he had been a Communist since his college days — but he pretended not to be one in order to deceive those whose support he needed.[2]

Another Communist confidence man was Ben Bella of Algeria. His cause was espoused as far back as 1957 in speeches by a young Senator named John F. Kennedy. After Kennedy was elected President, he invited Ben Bella to Washington. He is the only person in history ever to be welcomed to the United States with a 21-gun salute on the lawn of the White House. The next day Ben Bella went down to Havana and kissed Castro.[3] And one would have to be a Communist to kiss Castro!

One of the smoothest Communist confidence men was Sukarno. He "took" the United States for $2 billion — and then in 1965 stole most American-owned property in Indonesia and announced he was joining Red China, North Vietnam and North Korea in building an "anti-imperialist axis."[4]

The prevailing view in our nation's capital is that the Communists have used up their bag of tricks, that now we can trust them because they have "mellowed." This opinion cannot be supported by the facts. After so much practice in successfully cheating Americans so many times, the Soviets are ready now for the confidence game to end all confidence games.

The current Red confidence game is to trick the United States into believing we are in a period of *detente* — so we will believe we can safely accept a position as the No. 2 military power in the world today. *Detente* is the new sophisticated word for international "togetherness." It is fostered by much talk of peace, trade, and disarmament. Under cover of this detente, and having diverted our attention to Vietnam and small conventional weapons, the Reds are arming to the teeth with super-weapons for their new strike in the West.

History, logic and common sense all tell us that to rely on detente would be to rely on the same foolish hunch that President Roosevelt played in 1943. But some Americans, after they have dined on enough caviar and vodka, become victims of this confidence game.

The Tantrum

In May 1960, Khrushchev put on an act that was the envy of every Hollywood character actor. The stage was set for an Eisenhower-Khrushchev Summit Conference in Paris. The advance publicity had built up for months; lower-echelon diplomats were already on hand; the conference rooms were waiting. Then came one of the most sensational news events since World War II: an American U-2 spy plane was brought down over Russia.

Immediately Khrushchev went into a public tantrum. He insulted President Eisenhower. He insulted the United States. He torpedoed the Paris Summit Conference. For days, he filled the ears of the world with a non-stop diatribe against America.

Why did Khrushchev put on his act at that particular time? Soviet radar had been tracking the U-2 flights over Russia for 4 years; and U.S. intelligence *knew* that Khrushchev knew about them.

By May 1960, the Soviets had progressed far enough with the "serial" or mass production of ICBMs that they were ready to conceal a large number throughout Russia's huge territory. It was absolutely vital to Khrushchev to *hide* the location of these missiles — which were to be zeroed in on America — from U-2 or other U.S. spy-in-the-sky systems. Khrushchev's tantrum tactic worked like magic. It so terrorized U.S. liberals that they successfully pressured the Administration to cancel the U-2 flights over Russia. The curtain was pulled down on U.S. knowledge of Soviet offensive missiles for the next two years.

There is another important lesson for us in Khrushchev's tantrum. Hidden in the midst of many thousands of vituperative words in a 3-hour harangue on May 7, 1960, were 17 significant words. He described the American U-2 program as:

"an adventure to bring the course of history to a standstill, and to delay our inevitable victory."

How could a U-2 do this? Obviously, only if the Soviets had a plan to advance "the course of history" and to speed-up their "inevitable victory" *by preparations which aerial photography could prematurely expose.*

Khrushchev's slip should have been a clue to America that he must have a plan for a surprise attack by the secret deployment of strategic nuclear missiles. His slip was correctly interpreted in strategy seminars[5] but, as usual, attracted no official attention. Two years later, actual events demonstrated exactly how a U-2 could indeed "bring to a standstill the course of history" and delay the Soviets' "inevitable victory." In October 1962, a U-2 flight exposed Soviet preparations for a surprise attack on the U.S. from Cuba.

Therefore, history proves that (1) Khrushchev once did make a slip of the tongue which revealed his secret plan, and (2) it was correctly interpreted by strategists as exposing a Soviet plan for a surprise attack, but (3) the Administration ignored this clear warning until it was almost too late. If the Administration had acted with common sense, it could easily have prevented the shipment of Soviet missiles into Cuba. It could have mounted a blockade in time in a legal and peaceful manner.[6]

The solution of "the world's greatest mystery" shows that Khrushchev was forced to resign because of 3 slips of the tongue that shook the Kremlin. Can we learn the lesson of the tantrum, make sure that our Government takes warning from these slips, and then takes the necessary action?

Aesopian Language

Ever since Lenin, Communists have spoken to each other in what they call Aesopian language, that is, words which carry an activating message to Party members, and a paralyzing message to the free world. Khrushchev's famous speech of January 6, 1961, contains many examples of Aesopian language, such as:

"The fight for disarmament is an active fight against imperialism, for narrowing its war potential. The peoples must do everything to achieve the prohibition and destruction of nuclear weapons and all other weapons of wholesale annihilation. Peace will then be insured."

In Aesopian language, "imperialism" means the United States. "Disarmament" means narrowing the military strength — not of both sides — but of the U.S. alone, and it refers particularly to "nuclear weapons." "Peace," of course, means the condition *after* the Communists have conquered the world, as explained in the 1960 *Moscow Manifesto:*

"The victory of Socialism all over the world will completely remove the social and national causes of all wars."

Thus, the Reds deliberately use words which will put the West off-guard, while the Party faithful recognize these same words as a call to action.

Another example of Aesopian language is the Kremlin document that accused Khrushchev of "wrongly boasting the Soviet Union possesses a 'doomsday weapon' last month in meeting visiting Japanese lawmakers."[7] The impression is carefully planted that the Soviet Union possesses no such weapons; but what the statement actually says is that it was Khrushchev's boasting that was wrong.

Stop, Thief

Everyone knows that the easiest way for a purse snatcher to escape detection in a crowd is to yell loudly, "Stop, thief!" The Soviets use this tactic on a massive scale. They continually accuse the United States of preparing a surprise attack on them! This is effective for two reasons. First, it keeps America on the defensive — our diplomats must constantly protest that *we* have no aggressive designs. Second, it gives Kremlin spokesmen the opportunity to talk about surprise attack and thus, under cover of Aesopian language, they can spread their own war message to Party members.

There are many examples of the Soviet "Stop, thief" tactic. They accused the United States of cheating on the nuclear test ban all the time the Soviets were engaging in the greatest example of premeditated cheating in history. They accused us of aggression in Berlin at the very time they were preparing to build the Wall. They constantly accuse us of engaging in germ warfare, all the while they are racing ahead in chemical and biological weapons. They accuse us of aggression in Vietnam at the same time that they are shipping their surface-to-air missiles into Hanoi and arming the Viet Cong.

Credibility

The Soviet plan is designed to be so shocking to the non-Communist mind that, even if we prematurely discover it, we simply will not believe it. The Soviet plan is literally so horrible to contemplate that Americans reject the very idea. Even in the face of the historic fact that the Soviets did send their offensive missiles into Cuba, most Americans still believe: "The Soviets simply would not do such a thing!"

Just as Hitler discovered that it is much easier to put over a big lie than a little one, the Soviets discovered that it is easier to hide a big plot than a little one. If we discovered a Soviet plot to take over Panama or West Berlin, we would take action; but a Soviet plot to destroy the United States is literally too big a plot to believe.

The Soviets are also banking on the fact that the American people will refuse to believe the plot because, if they did believe it, they would feel obliged to pull out of their lethargy and their leisure, and do something about it. Americans say to themselves: "Perhaps the Communists really do plan to conquer the world, but certainly such a far-out plan is not sufficient motive for deliberately plotting to kill 149 million Americans! After all, we are nice people (which we certainly are) and we have never done the Russians any harm (which is certainly true)."

The official *Moscow Manifesto* of 1960 explains the motive behind the Kremlin's strategy:

"War is a constant companion of capitalism. The system of exploitation of man by man and the system of extermination of man by man are two aspects of the capitalist system. Imperialism has already inflicted two devastating world wars on mankind and now threatens to plunge it into an even more terrible catastrophe.

"Monstrous means of mass annihilation and destruction have been developed which, if used in a new war, can cause unheard of destruction to entire countries, and reduce key centers of world industry and culture to ruins. Such a war would bring death and suffering to hundreds of millions of people, among them people in countries not involved in it. Imperialism spells grave danger to the whole of mankind.

"The peoples must be more vigilant than ever. As long as imperialism exists there will be soil for wars of aggression. The peoples of all countries know that the danger of a new world war still persists. U.S. imperialism is the main force of aggression and war."[8]

In Aesopian language, this says that the only way to save the world from hundreds of millions of casualties, to save even neutral countries, to save centers of production and culture — to avert World War III with its "terrible catastrophe" for mankind — is to destroy "U.S. imperialism."

Thus, under this solemn declaration by the 81 Communist Parties of the World, a surprise strike at the United States would be for the self preservation of all Communist countries, of mankind, of industry, and of culture.

But what of the experts, such as Herman Kahn, who tell us we need not fear a nuclear Pearl Harbor? Kahn did not arrive at this conclusion by logic, or evidence, or even by himself. This would have required him to eat many thousand brilliantly-chosen words in his own masterpiece, *On Thermonuclear War*. Kahn proved in that opus that an aggressor could win through a massive surprise nuclear attack; he proved it so thoroughly that it would be impossible for him to disprove it now. So he thought of a clever dodge. In his 1965 book, *On Escalation*, he bases his new position on "several polls" of nuclear strategists and scientists and claims that the consensus is that it is unlikely that the Soviets "would start an all-out general war. . . ."

The mere fact that the consensus thinks an attack unlikely is *not* an optimistic omen because this "consensus" has *never* been right about any major Soviet move. This is the same consensus that assured us the Soviets would never send offensive missiles to Cuba. Roberta Wohlstetter, who from her staff position at the Rand Corporation and as a writer for *Foreign Affairs* should be in a position to know, says there was no articulate dissent from the consensus of experts who did *not* believe the Soviets would sneak their offensive missiles into Cuba.[9]

Can we afford to gamble our lives on the "consensus" which has never before been right about Soviet intentions? What is the secret Soviet strategy?

chapter V

PEACE OF THE GRAVE

"Enjoy your dream of peace just one more day.
. . . Hawaii, you will be caught like a rat in a
trap."

These were the words of Japanese Admiral
Matome Ugaki, Yamamoto's Chief of Staff, on
December 6, 1941.[1]

This was how the cocksure Japanese launched
their vicious attack on Pearl Harbor, dealing the
United States the greatest single military disaster
in its history. It was an attack on an unsuspecting
America, dreaming of peace — while both experts
and amateurs relaxed in the twin defense myths
of that day: that Pearl Harbor was impregnable,
the Gibraltar of the Pacific; and that Japan would
be deterred from launching a surprise attack
because of fear of devastating U.S. retaliation.

Why was America caught so completely by surprise? Our Government had received many warnings in advance of the attack. On January 27,
1941, our Ambassador to Japan, Joseph C. Grew,
sent this communique to our State Department:
". . . the Japanese, in case of a break with the U.S.,
are planning to go all out in a surprise mass attack
on Pearl Harbor."[2] The FBI had warned of frequent messages which were sent to Tokyo from
the Japanese consulate at Honolulu telling of the
presence and absence of American warships at

Pearl Harbor. The House Committee on Un-American Activities had reported espionage by Japanese fishing vessels.

Most important, Navy Captain Laurance Safford had broken the Japanese codes and given the Pentagon, the White House and the State Department the top-secret Japanese messages to their Ambassadors that war with the United States would begin on December 7.[3] Looking at all the evidence which was available to the Roosevelt Administration prior to Pearl Harbor, it seems impossible that these warnings could have been ignored.

A generation later we have equally clear warnings, but again our Government is failing to act. This time the price will be not thousands but many millions of American lives, not only the boys in uniform but also their families at home, because this time the weapons of surprise attack are 100 million times more powerful.

All the evidence screams the terrible conclusion that the Soviet strategy is *Make a Noise in Vietnam, but STRIKE FROM SPACE.* The Soviets deliberately trapped us in Vietnam to divert our attention and resources to a guerrilla-conventional war and away from the nuclear threat in space.

How Do We Know?

Since 1957 the Soviets have been engaged in a gigantic research and weapons program to build up special capability for a massive attack. They have high-power warheads and tremendous rocket thrust. It is naive to think the Soviets developed this capability accidentally, or as a result of peaceful scientific progress. The Soviets carried out an ambitious propaganda campaign to prevent the U.S. from testing nuclear weapons. They tricked us into the first test ban and betrayed it after months of secret preparations. Then, the U.S. signed the Moscow Test Ban Treaty, which guaranteed the permanence of the U.S.S.R. strategic lead in nuclear super-weapons, and froze the United States in second place.

The only rational explanation for the Cuban missile crisis in 1962 is that Khrushchev decided to advance his timetable, take the tremendous risks involved, and launch his massive surprise attack from Cuba. The missiles he shipped into Cuba were capable of doing just that. The nearness of Cuba gave Khrushchev the perfect opportunity for a no-warning attack — the strike would be upon us before a single bomber could be launched or the countdown completed on a single one of the liquid-fuel ICBMs we then possessed. We were saved from disaster "only by the grace of God and an aerial photograph."

The solution to "the world's greatest mystery" proves that Khrushchev was forced to resign because he had made too many slips revealing the secret Kremlin plan for a surprise nuclear attack. This solution demonstrates also that Brezhnev and Kosygin's policy is "Khrushchevism without Khrushchev."

Brezhnev and Kosygin were the only two Presidium-level co-conspirators with Khrushchev in the plot to destroy the U.S. by a missile strike from Cuba. Brezhnev's close connection with the Soviet space program is a significant clue that the Kremlin's next strike will be from space — a *Space Cuba*.

Two independent items of direct testimony confirm the fact that the Soviets are planning a surprise nuclear attack against the United States. In 1962 a 450-page book called *Soviet Military Strategy* was published in the Soviet Union. Edited by Marshal V. D. Sokolovskii and 13 other senior officers of the Red Army including 9 generals, it is a "Mein Kampf" blueprint for burying the United States under a massive all-out surprise attack just as soon as the Soviets achieve sufficient nuclear superiority to get away with it without incurring major damage to the Soviet Union.

This remarkable book was allowed to be published and taken out of Russia because it was written with a double protection against it being understood by the West. First, much of the meaning was covered with Aesopian language. Second, it *reverses* the aggressor and the victim of the surprise attack! It devotes page after page to asserting that the U.S. is plotting a preventive war against the U.S.S.R. By this ruse, the Soviet military leaders are able to describe in detail how a surprise nuclear attack must be planned, prepared for, and conducted so that the aggressor will reduce his own damage to the minimum. Here is one of many examples:

> "The question is this: If general nuclear war is dangerous to both sides, then what must be done so that it can lead to the attainment of the desired objectives, i.e., the destruction of the enemy with the least possible losses and destruc-

tion for oneself? The American imperialists . . . answer this question as follows: First, sharply step up the arms race, especially nuclear missiles and nuclear space weapons; and second, achieve surprise. The first measure must assure overwhelming quantitative superiority over the enemy in the most advanced strategic weapons, primarily missiles and nuclear and space weapons, in order to make possible a continuing policy of intimidation toward the Soviet Union."[4] Now try rereading this passage with the names reversed, and you will see the Soviets' own strategy against America.

The other piece of unexpected evidence about Soviet strategy came from the 1963 trial of Colonel Stig Wennerstroem, who surely ranks as one of the most successful spies of all time. A colonel in the Swedish army, a suavely handsome aviator, a longtime air attache in Washington, D. C., he secretly passed Swedish, U.S. and NATO secrets to the Soviets for 15 years. Wennerstroem was so valuable a spy for the Kremlin that he held the secret rank of Soviet Major General, was awarded several medals, and allowed to accumulate $100,-000 in back pay in Moscow, in addition to cash handouts of $750 to $1,000 per month. After a sensational trial in Sweden, Wennerstroem was jailed for life as a Soviet spy.

Much valuable information came to light during Wennerstroem's trial. He testified that, since the 1950s, the Soviets have given the highest priority to rockets and nuclear warheads, at the expense of every other economic and even military consideration. He testified that, in his spying for the Soviets, his bosses told him not to bother to steal U.S. secrets of chemical and biological warfare, because the Soviets knew they were "far ahead in these fields." He was such a daring and successful spy that he would often — at official functions — hand over microfilm and other secrets to the Soviet general who was his underground boss. Wennerstroem testified that he even handed U.S. secrets to this Soviet general inside the Pentagon itself![5]

Have the Soviets the capability of launching a crippling strike from space on the United States?

In March 1965 General Curtis LeMay, recently retired as Air Force Chief of Staff, warned that Russia might be developing space weapons that would give them military superiority over the United States.[6] Also in March, Air Force General Thomas S. Power, for 7 years head of the U.S. Strategic Air Command, warned that Americans "may wake up one morning" and find a number of nuclear-armed Soviet satellites "floating in stationary orbits over every part of the United States."[7]

On July 4, 1965, Communist Party Chief Brezhnev, in a Kremlin speech, declared that the Soviets possess "orbital rockets." Two weeks later the Soviets launched the heaviest space craft payload ever orbited. Named Proton I, it weighed 26,500 pounds — more than 10,000 pounds heavier than the biggest previous Soviet satellite. Only one day earlier, the Soviets had orbited 5 unmanned satellites with a single rocket. On September 3 they launched 5 more the same way. In the light of these actual demonstrations of massive rocket-thrust capability, plus the fact that they have had 4 years to multiply the 100-megaton warhead capability they demonstrated by tests in October 1961, and to improve their yield/weight ratio, no responsible authority can deny the possibility that the Soviets possess "gigaton" warheads, orbital bombs, and multiple warheads for super-missiles.

This would mean that the Soviets have the capability to accomplish their world conquest by strategic nuclear weapons. *First,* the attack against the United States could be delivered with complete surprise — with "zero warning" — because an orbital bomber carrying a warhead in the gigaton range does not need to be deorbited before the button is pushed. *Second,* the attack could destroy or render inoperative up to 90% of U.S. strategic retaliatory forces. Our so-called "invulnerable" land-based missiles are not de-signed to withstand such unprecedented explosive power, and all our remaining bombers (except the few on airborne alert) are vulnerable with less than 15 minutes' warning; nor could our com-munications, command and control networks func-tion after such an attack. *Third,* the attack would be "genocidal," that is, the entire population of the United States would be the prime target. This genocidal result could be re-insured 30 minutes later by a follow-on attack with multiple-warhead missiles, ideal for annihilating entire population centers, and still later by their manned bombers which, unlike missiles, can seek out undestroyed areas.

Would the Soviets really do such a terrible thing? Is it possible that man could be so depraved as to conceive and carry out a plot to destroy America by a surprise strike from space? To the Soviets, there are many valid reasons why they think this plan is justifiable. From the Soviets' point of view, in Khrushchev's colorful language, they "would be slobbering idiots" if they did not![8]

(1) To the Soviets, this would be preventive war. It would prevent nuclear damage to the Soviet Union and insure world "peace" on their terms. (2) The Soviets' goal is world conquest. They cannot conquer the world if the U.S. remains a super power. According to Communist doctrine, whatever stands in the way of reaching that objective must be eliminated. (3) The Reds look upon the mere existence of a free economy as a threat because it offers people an alternative. They know they cannot compete in agriculture or industry. This is why Khrushchev called West Berlin "a bone in my throat" and then built the Berlin Wall. This is why Red China hates the mere existence of Formosa, which has worked up to such prosperity it no longer accepts U.S. economic or agricultural aid.

Wouldn't a surprise strike on the U.S. be prohibitively expensive to the Soviets? On the contrary, it would cost very little — and in return they would get the world — and all its wealth. The Soviets already have made the big investment in H-bombs and space weapons; after wiping out the United States, they would need only a few to control the rest of the world by nuclear blackmail.

The Soviets haven't the slightest intention of starting a *bilateral* thermonuclear war. The surprise attack they have so long and so expensively prepared for is designed for the specific purpose of *preventing* a nuclear exchange. It takes two to fight a war. Their surprise attack, their "space Pearl Harbor," is calculated to win with one massive strike from space — after which there will be few American people to fight back; and those who are left would consider it irrational to retaliate against the Russian people (who had no part in the decision to strike us) with any of our weapons which *might* survive.

When will the Soviets carry out their surprise strike? Since 1962 they have had the big warheads that can do the job. They now are waiting until the time is right, until they can minimize the retaliatory damage to the Soviet Union and, in the meantime, feather their nest with wheat, chemical plants and other goodies from the United States. Up to now, the Soviets have been restrained by our retaliatory capability. As soon as the Soviets think that they are strong enough and we are weak enough so that they will suffer no more damage than they had in World War II, the time will be ripe. Time is on the side of the Soviets because they are using it and we are not.

Isn't it more likely that the Soviets would give us a surrender ultimatum so they could take America intact? No. An ultimatum would eliminate surprise on which all Soviet strategy depends. The Soviets cannot afford to give us a warning and thereby risk damage to themselves. Furthermore, the Soviets don't want the job of governing a distant and defeated America. It would create too many problems of administration, transportation, and police. Europe is within their reach, and will require most of their effort.

George Kennan, who originated many of the "soft" U.S. policies toward the Soviet Union, recently prepared for the Council on Foreign Relations, a study entitled "On Dealing With the Communist World." His theme was that we should never oust the Communist Government of the Soviet Union, because it would be impossible for us to govern or administer the area; and he gave a convincing list of reasons why. Ironically, these reasons, which would certainly apply to the Kremlin's trying to govern the American people, convincingly support the thesis that the Soviet dictators would far rather have us dead than Red. It would be much better from the Soviet point of view, to wipe out the United States, and then they would have the world.

The liberals have tried to explain away the famous Khrushchev quote

"History is on our side. We will bury you."

by saying he didn't really mean it literally, that he merely planned to defeat capitalism economically or in other peaceful pursuits. Such an interpretation is contrary to the plain fact that no Communist regime is able to compete economically with the United States — and Khrushchev knew this all too well. Besides, he was always a man who said what he meant and meant what he said.

Burying the United States was a favorite theme of Khrushchev; he repeated it often, most recently in 1963 when he said:

". . . we want — not only want but have dug — quite a deep hole, and shall exert efforts to dig this hole deeper and bury the capitalist system forever."[10]

When Khrushchev threatened to bury us, he meant it literally and emphatically — he meant that he planned to bury us under a hydrogen holocaust. The new Kremlin bosses have echoed this same morbid refrain. Soviet Defense Minister Malinovsky threatened that Vietnam could explode into a "great war" in which "the imperialist system will find its grave."[11] As they plot the space age equivalent of Pearl Harbor, the Soviets must have thoughts as the Japanese had: "America, enjoy your dreams of peace just one more day. You will be caught like a rat in a trap." Under the Kremlin plan for "peace," our only "peace" would be the peace of the grave.

The "Frame of Mind"

Can it be possible that the Soviets are planning a surprise strike from space and our Government doesn't know it — or hasn't prepared for it?

Remember the classic examples of Pearl Harbor and the Cuban missile crisis. Both happened because the men in our Government closed their minds to the plain evidence before their eyes. Prior to Pearl Harbor, Secretary of War Henry Stimson even refused to read the decoded Japanese messages which forecast the attack because, he said: "Gentlemen don't read each other's mail."[12]

In 1962, millions of Americans knew the Kremlin had shipped offensive missiles into Cuba before our Government would believe the far greater amounts of evidence it had long possessed. The Senate Preparedness Investigating Subcommittee reported that the Kennedy Administration's almost-fatal delay in believing the evidence was due to

"the predisposition of the intelligence community to the philosophical conviction that it would be incompatible with Soviet policy to introduce strategic missiles into Cuba."[13]

A far more chilling explanation of why the Government is so slow in recognizing evidence of surprise attacks appeared — of all places — in *Foreign Affairs,* prestigious publication of the Council on Foreign Relations, in an article by Rand staff member and liberal expert Roberta Wohlstetter:

"Once a predisposition about an opponent's behavior becomes settled, it is very hard to shake. In this case [Cuba], it was reinforced not only by expert authority but also by the knowledge both conscious and unconscious that the White House had set down a policy for relaxation of tension with the East.

"This policy background was much more subtle in its influence than documents or diplomatic experience. For when an official policy or hypothesis is laid down, it tends to obscure alternative hypotheses, and to lead to overemphasis of the data that support it, particularly in a situation of increasing tension, when it is important not to 'rock the boat.' "[14]

Translated into forthright English, this means that a strong-willed President, surrounded by liberals who have sold him on "detente," exercises an irresistible "brainwashing" type of influence over all those who handle our military and foreign policy and gather our intelligence. If the President's policy is based on the theory that the Soviets are our friends, that the Kremlin dictators are "responsible" statesmen working for "peaceful coexistence," that any hostile words or actions should be ignored because they result solely from Soviet competition with Red China — then our intelligence "experts," the Pentagon Whiz Kids, and even the generals and admirals hand-picked by McNamara for top military positions, are all rendered incapable of objectively evaluating the evidence of a surprise Soviet attack. Mrs. Wohlstetter then gives this stern warning to her fellow liberals of how they look from the vantage of hindsight:

> "It is this prior frame of mind, now changed, that we forget most easily in retrospect. And it is this above all that makes every past surprise nearly unintelligible — and *inexplicable except perhaps as criminal folly or conspiracy.*
>
> "The genuine analogies between Pearl Harbor and Cuba should not obscure the important difference. A study of the Pearl Harbor case makes it clear that the problem of *getting warning of an impending nuclear raid today is much harder than the problem of detecting the Japanese attack some 20 years ago.*"[15] (emphasis added)

If President Kennedy and his entire staff of civilian and military advisors had so brainwashed themselves into a "frame of mind" that they were completely unable to interpret the evidence about Soviet missiles in Cuba — can we expect Lyndon Johnson to do any better with the evidence of a strike from space?

But the evidence is there. If America is to survive in freedom, Americans must face this evidence — and we must also make our President face it.

Now let us see what is the actual response by men in our Government to the Soviet strategy of strike from space.

chapter **VI**

EISENHOWER'S WARNING

In his Farewell Address on January 17, 1961, President Dwight D. Eisenhower warned us about a danger which had not previously been mentioned publicly by any American leader:

"Yet in holding scientific research and discovery in respect, as we should, we must also be alert to the equal and opposite *danger that public policy could itself become the captive of a scientific-technological elite.*" (emphasis added)

Eisenhower's warning has consistently been given the silent treatment by the liberal press. What did he mean?

Throughout the 1940s and the 1950s, one of the sure ways to be "in" with the fashionable intellectuals was to talk of the tremendous *rate* of growth inside the Soviet Union. True, said the liberals, the Soviets didn't have a fraction of the automobiles or bathtubs we had, but the *rate* of growth was so remarkable that the Soviets would soon pass us in all fields including industry, agriculture, education and military strength. For 30 years this myth — born of a tender sympatico with the "great Socialist experiment" — was popular in all liberal circles.

Beginning in 1956, in the classrooms of the National War College and in seminars held for top-echelon bureaucrats, U.S. Kremlinologists began to predict that the day was approaching when the Soviet Union would pass the United States in the technology of weapons of war. These lecturers projected the comparative curves of Soviet and American scientific progress and showed that, although the United States was then out in front, the Soviets would pass us in the 1960s. The intellectuals had it figured that the Soviets would inevitably win the arms race because the U.S. could not, or would not, spend a large enough percentage of our gross national product and of our Federal budget to stay ahead.

In 1959, leading U.S. Kremlinologist George Kennan publicly and explicitly expressed his belief that the Soviet system was so vastly superior to the American system, that we simply could not compete. Kennan's words are significant because he became one of President Kennedy's most influential advisers on U.S. policy relating to the Soviet Union as well as his Ambassador to Yugoslavia. Kennan's words are far more important than if they represented only his thinking. He has frequently been the pivotal force in molding U.S. policy, and he is really the theoretician of the scientific-technological-intellectual elite which for the last 5 years has held "captive" U.S. defense and foreign policies. Here is how these people feel about America and the Soviet Union:

> "If you ask me — as a historian, let us say — whether a country in the state this country is in today: with no highly developed sense of national purpose, with the overwhelming accent of life on personal comfort and amusement, with

a dearth of public services and a surfeit of privately sold gadgetry, with a chaotic transportation system . . . with an educational system where quality has been extensively sacrificed to quantity, and with insufficient social discipline to keep even its major industries functioning without grievous interruptions [a steel strike was then pending] — if you ask me whether such a country has, over the long run, good chances of competing with a purposeful, serious and disciplined society such as that of the Soviet Union, I must say that the answer is 'no.' "[1]

When it became apparent that the Soviets were *not* winning the economic race, and the contrast between our surpluses and Red shortages was obvious even to the Socialists, the scientific-technological elite, of whom President Eisenhower warned, still placed their bets on the U.S.S.R. They concluded, with some logic, that the very fact Russia did not have mass production of automobiles, telephones and television was proof that the Kremlin had put everything into nuclear weapons at the expense of consumer, government, and even other military considerations. Because they knew the awful power of the nuclear Frankenstein they had created, the scientists concluded that America faced a future of defeat and probable devastation.

The Gravediggers

Thus, over a period of several years, there developed a group of scientists, professors and bureaucrats who came to believe that, since the Soviets were bound to win the arms race, the only way the U.S. could avoid nuclear war was to disarm unilaterally so the Soviets would feel they did not need to attack. Whereas Sputnik encouraged the American people and the politicians to try to catch up, it only further convinced this group that we could never win and therefore nuclear disarmament was the only way to avoid destruction.

This scientific and intellectual elite are the people we call the "gravediggers." By working for unilateral disarmament, they are truly digging our graves so the men in the Kremlin can fulfill their repeated threats to bury us.

The official unveiling of this plan took place at Asilomar, California on April 29, 1960 when a New York investment banker named Paul H. Nitze presented a detailed plan to scrap U.S. nuclear strength so drastic that it would enable the Soviets to pass us quickly in the strategic arms race. He argued that the U.S. should not even be a close second-best, but should retain only "purely retaliatory" weapons. Of course, that would make us much weaker than the Soviets, *but* "it would be *hoped*" that the Soviets would follow our example and do likewise.

Meanwhile, in 1957 a group of scientists which centered around Dr. Eugene Rabinowitch, editor of the *Bulletin for Atomic Scientists,* and later included Dr. Linus Pauling, organized to promote nuclear disarmament. With Lord Bertrand Russell issuing the invitations, and Cyrus Eaton footing the bill, the Pugwash Conferences were launched.[2] As described by Rabinowitch, these Pugwash Conferences represent the "gradual abandonment of the idea of large propaganda meetings issuing ringing appeals for peace and disarmament, and acceptance of small and large confidential conferences (with key scientists and government advisers) as promising greater practical results."

Are the Pugwash Conferences important? Dr. Rabinowitch quotes with obvious delight the remark by one Soviet participant:

"I heard that the Pugwash Conferences are officially unofficial, but now I see they are unofficially official."[3]

Because of the importance and influence of the men who attend, the Pugwash Conferences have become the fountainhead of propaganda for nuclear disarmament. Their sinister influence was first publicly exposed by the American Security Council's *Washington Report* on March 14, 1961. It revealed the existence of a secret Report of the Senate Internal Security Subcommittee which documented the twin facts that the Pugwash Conferences were a new Communist design for the subversion of the U.S. scientific elite, and were using this elite within the U.S. Government to influence the policies of the Kennedy-Johnson Administration toward nuclear disarmament. Despite tremendous Administration pressure to suppress the Senate report in order to protect Pugwash from exposure, the Senate Report was finally published.[4]

The most important of the 13 Pugwash Conferences was the one held in Moscow in November-December 1960, attended by Dr. Walt W. Rostow and Dr. Jerome B. Wiesner who, within a few weeks, became high policy-making officials of the new Kennedy-Johnson Administration. Following their lead, other gravediggers and Pugwashers flocked onto the Government payroll and began making policy. Paul Nitze became Assistant Secretary of Defense and later was promoted to Secretary of the Navy. Soon their plans were revealed.

Out of Their Own Mouths

The gravediggers' plans to dismantle American military strength *unilaterally* can be documented both by their actions and by their official and semi-official documents.

Most important is Secretary of Defense Robert Strange McNamara, whose own official testimony and public statements reveal that his policies are carrying out the unilateral disarmament plans of the gravediggers and reducing our strategic nuclear striking power by 90%.[5]

Walt Whitman Rostow, the Pugwasher who became Chairman of the State Department Policy Planning Council, wrote his secret Rostow Report which laid down the "no-win" policy of the Kennedy-Johnson Administration and said we must abandon our first-strike weapons in order to allay Soviet suspicions.

Roswell Leavitt Gilpatric, longtime No. 2 man in the Pentagon, published in *Foreign Affairs* in April 1964 a specific proposal for U.S. unilateral disarmament just as drastic as the Nitze Asilomar Proposal. He is also the author of the Gilpatric Report, a 1965 study on nuclear problems kept secret from the American people.[6] His proposals would drag U.S. policy down from "no-win" to "can't-win" to "sure-lose."

William C. Foster, Chief of the U.S. Arms Control and Disarmament Agency set up in 1961, bears primary responsibility for the many studies prepared or paid for by his Agency. These include the notorious Phoenix Study which cost $78,600. Many of its recommendations have already been put into effect. Its proposals for unilateral disarmament are so extreme that they even recommend the "unification" of the United States and the Soviet Union. Fortunately the gravediggers have not been able to put that idea into practice yet, but that doesn't keep them from trying!

The Liberal Papers, a paperback book sponsored by James Roosevelt and 35 other Democratic Congressmen, endorsed unilateral disarmament, "rather Red than dead", U.S. foreign aid to Red China, and inviting the Soviets to plug in on our DEW line.

Dean Rusk issued *State Department Publication 7277* calling for the 3-stage abolition of our Army, Navy, Air Force and nuclear weapons.

George Wildman Ball, Under Secretary of State who carries the ball for the gravediggers in the economic field, authored the still-secret Ball Report calling for a vast increase of trade with Communist countries, even in strategic items.

Jerome Wiesner, the Pugwasher who became top science adviser to the Kennedy-Johnson Administration, spread the new nuclear line in his book, *Where Science and Politics Meet,* and in publications such as *Scientific American.*[7]

McGeorge Bundy, Special Assistant to the President for National Security Affairs, spread the nuclear line in publications such as *Foreign Affairs* that U.S. "nuclear strength can be provocative."[8]

Averell Harriman, the only participant in the Yalta Conference who *still* defends that sellout, the architect of the tragic Laos coalition, crawled to Moscow and came home with the Moscow Test Ban Treaty of 1963 which the U.S. Joint Chiefs said froze the U.S. in second-place in super-nuclear weapons. In July 1965 he was in Moscow again to discuss disarmament with Kosygin.[9]

George Kennan was the earliest influential advocate of nuclear disarmament and of a pledge — by the U.S. only, of course — of "no first use" of nuclear weapons. In 1961 he came out with a book which pompously pooh-poohed the very idea that "the Russians want universal power, and will be likely to take over the world if we fail to do this or that." He pontificated that the Kremlin could not extend its power beyond "those areas which it is able to dominate with its own armed forces, and without involving impossible lines of communication. . . . There are geographic limits to the possibilities of military occupation."[10] The following year, the Soviets disproved Kennan by stretching their communications line 10,000 miles for the round-trip deployment of troops and strategic missiles to Cuba.

The importance of Dr. Harold Brown as Secretary of the Air Force was described this way by

a distinguished observer of Pentagon policies:
"During the past few years, at Congressional
hearings, whenever Defense Secretary Robert
Strange McNamara wanted to cancel an important strategic weapon, the one man he
always produced to learnedly support his thesis
was Dr. Harold Brown, then the Pentagon's
Director of Research and Engineering. Now,
with all that this signifies, he has been nominated
Secretary of the Air Force, the very service
which has been leading the fight against this
policy."[11]

North American Aviation, Inc. prepared a study
in April 1965 called "Factors Operative in a Post-
Arms Control Situation." This document, paid for
under Air Force Contract No. 49(638)-1411,
leaked out because someone forgot to stamp it
classified, and one employee decided the American
people should know what specific disarmament
plans and "scenarios" are already being acted out.

Senator William Fulbright, chief spokesman on
Capitol Hill for gravedigger ideas, wrote his
notorious *Memorandum* and chimes in constantly
with such aid-our-enemy statements as (1) the
Communists have a "right" to block refugees flee-
ing to West Berlin — made two weeks before the
Soviets built the Berlin Wall,[12] (2) we should
accept the "continued existence" of Castro in
Cuba,[13] and (3) we should make "major
concessions" in Vietnam.[14]

Walter Lippmann, who bugles retreat in every
crisis with the Communists, wrote a column during
the Cuban confrontation which gave Khrushchev
the idea that he could demand and get with-

drawal of U.S. missiles from Turkey in exchange for his withdrawal from Cuba.[15]

"Study Fair"

As an illustration of the content of gravedigger Government documents, let us examine the one called *Study Fair*.[16] Although written in 1963, it was successfully kept secret from the American people all during the 1964 election campaign. It was first discovered and reported by the American Security Council *in 1965*.

Fair is an acronym which stands for Focus on Arms Information and Reassurance. What a misnomer! There is nothing *fair* or *reassuring* about it, but the *information* it gives about the plans of the gravediggers makes it one of the most important secret documents ever to come to light.

Study Fair takes up the question of what information we should have about the Soviets, concluding that there is "significant danger in information which is *too informative*"! It is "destabilizing" and "unsettling" to know too much about the enemy. It is more "stabilizing" to have "*in*accurate information" which shows that the enemy cannot or does not want to attack us. Even if the Soviet Union really "*is* about to strike" us by surprise, it is dangerous for us to know this and we should "minimize" the information.

Study Fair gives detailed plans on how we should *reduce* the information we have about Soviet plans. When we have observation systems, they should have "strictly *limited* capabilities." We should install "automatic measures for *delaying* the transmission of information" about Soviet war plans. During a crisis, we should *"turn the (U-2) cameras off"* so we will not be nervous about the movements of the enemy's missiles and aircraft. We should even give the Soviets a *"veto"* over what information is transmitted to our Government from various intelligence-gathering sources!

Study Fair also addresses itself to what information the Soviets should have about us. To the Soviets, we should "transmit only *reassuring* information . . . which suggests first strike weakness." If a crisis occurs and the Soviets get jittery, we should "reassure the Soviets that no Polaris submarines were within firing range of the U.S.S.R." If the Soviets get nervous anyway, *Study Fair* says we should give the Soviets the right *to order our* Polaris submarines to "surface and make their positions known."

How crackpotty can you get? In ancient days, the Roman emperors used to call in certain soothsayers and ask their advice. These seers would open up a chicken and, after studying the entrails, advise the emperor what to do. This ancient method of policy planning was sane and logical compared to having our defense policy guided by *Study Fair* and similar gravedigger treatises circulated at top echelons in our Government.

But let us focus a little closer on *Study Fair*. The U.S. taxpayers paid $19,000 for this fantastic report. It was co-sponsored by the U.S. Arms Control and Disarmament Agency, the Department of Defense, and U.S. Naval Ordnance. The principal author of *Study Fair* was a physicist named Dr.

John Phelps, one of the elite scientists who attended the Moscow Pugwash Conference. Only a very limited number of copies of *Study Fair* were printed and they circulated only among top-level policy makers in our Government. It was never intended to be read by the American people and in fact was successfully kept secret for nearly two years. Pugwasher Phelps is really saying — in gravedigger code language:

Fellow gravediggers, lend me your ears. The American people must never discover evidence that the Soviets are planning a surprise strike from space. We must keep reassuring them that this is impossible, and we must distort information so they won't find out. We must reassure the Soviets that, under no circumstances, will the U.S. use any nuclear weapons even in self defense.

In analyzing *Study Fair*, Lt. Gen. Arthur G. Trudeau said:

"Don't be deceived that these studies are merely think pieces. I've seen too many come to fruition to be fooled by this argument."[17]

Study Fair is only one of dozens of official and semi-official documents circulated at high Government levels, but kept secret from the American people whose taxes financed them. An objective reading of these documents brings us to the inescapable conclusion that the gravediggers have convicted themselves by their own words that they are in fact working for:

1) the immediate and rapid unilateral dismantling of American strategic military strength,

2) a deliberate campaign to deceive the American people about comparative U.S. and Soviet strength.

The gravediggers are not stupid men; they are highly educated and many of them are scientists. The ultra-elite among them are referred to in inner circles as the "Harvard-MIT Axis." They are not naive; they know the history of Soviet duplicity and they know the Soviet strategy is to strike without warning. They simply could not believe their own foolish statements that, if the U.S. disarms, the Soviets will follow our lead and disarm too.

Why then do the gravediggers not "level" with the American people? Why do they go to such lengths to hide from the American people the truth about a Soviet strike from space? Why do they warn each other that it is dangerous for the American people to have information about the Soviets which is "too informative"?

Why do they take extra pains to "reassure" the Soviets we will not use our weapons — even in self defense?

What is the hidden truth about gravediggers' plan for peace? Is it something so shocking that no one has yet dared say it?

chapter **VII**

SIX CURTAINS OF CONCEALMENT

If the gravediggers really have such evil designs, why don't the American people know about them? Why isn't this sensational news headlined on the front pages and blasted from radio and television?

Coercion

The majority of the men who understand nuclear strategy are in our military services and therefore effectively muzzled by the *Fulbright Memorandum*. This directive, first exposed on August 2, 1961,[1] initiated an Administration policy which banned the military from all anti-Communist activities, even from mentioning "the Communist challenge" in speeches.[2] Educational anti-Communist programs in the Armed Forces were eliminated. The Kennedy-Johnson Administration had no scruples about taking reprisals against any military man who violated Fulbright's directive. Military men learned that, in order to keep their jobs or receive promotions, they would have to conform to Administration policies, particularly about the cold war.

The *Fulbright Memorandum,* thus put into effect by a politically-minded Administration, was a ready-made weapon in the hands of the gravediggers. They used the *Memorandum's* policies to silence effectively most of the men who are capable of interpreting to the American people the real meaning of the gravediggers' strategic and foreign policies.[3] Under the ruthless rule of Robert Strange McNamara, every man of national or international reputation has been ousted or retired from the Joint Chiefs of Staff: Arthur Radford, Arleigh Burke, Curtis LeMay, Thomas D. White. McNamara has so downgraded the influence and authority of their replacements that they are known as the "Five Silent Men." As described by Congressman Craig Hosmer, senior minority member of the Joint Committee on Atomic Energy:

> "The work of Washington's disarmers is being made easier by the seemingly calculated elimination of top military spokesmen capable of communicating authoritatively with the American public. . . . No successors have been permitted to develop public prominence."[4]

Time described McNamara's personnel policy like this:

> "The new Joint Chiefs seem ideally suited to the requirements of Defense Secretary Robert McNamara, who personally selected each. No Defense Secretary in history has ever asserted Pentagon control like McNamara. The men he has chosen . . . have much in common. . . . All may be expected to state their policy views candidly — and then to support, at least in public, any decision made by McNamara and the President."[5]

The TFX contract award was used to teach the military the ruthless penalty for disagreeing with their civilian bosses. The Boeing plane had been evaluated by all experts and responsible military chiefs as vastly superior to the General Dynamics plane.[6] But McNamara, on the basis of figures he allegedly "carried in his head" and could not produce anywhere else for General Accounting Office Investigators, awarded the $6.5 billion contract to General Dynamics, whose plant just happened to be in Lyndon Johnson's home state. Admiral George W. Anderson, who testified truthfully before the Senate Committee on the superiority of the Boeing plane, was without warning let out of his top job as Chief of Naval Operations and forced into retirement after only a 2-year term, whereas 4 years had previously been the minimum and his predecessor had served 6 years. General Curtis LeMay, who also testified on the greater merits of the Boeing plane, was reappointed as Chief of Staff of the Air Force for an additional term of only one year — just long enough to keep him muzzled through the 1964 election.

In 1963 the only military men who dared even partially to oppose the Moscow Test Ban Treaty were Admiral George Anderson and Generals Thomas Power, Curtis LeMay, and Arthur Trudeau, all of whom were quickly retired. On the other hand, those who "buttered up" their civilian bosses could hope for career rewards. *Time* revealed that the new Chairman of the Joint Chiefs of Staff, Earle G. Wheeler, had

> "won McNamara's favor by his outspoken advocacy of the nuclear test ban treaty, trekking to Capitol Hill to rebut point by point the doubts

expressed by the Air Force's LeMay."[7]

A life-long habit of obedience, a genuine loyalty to superiors, and a true dedication to civilian supremacy under the Constitution of the United States, prevent military men on active duty from giving effective warning to the American people. There is no evidence that the Chiefs of Staff campaigned to secure their high offices — or that they have ever acted as "yes-men," even if McNamara hoped that they would. But they are good soldiers as well as patriotic Americans; they cannot speak out against Administration policies.

What about *retired* officers? Why don't they speak out? One reason generally unknown to the public is that they are all still subject to court-martial — and the Uniform Code of Military Justice says it is a court-martial offense, for which the punishment could be dismissal from the Service (with loss of retirement annuity, regardless of the years of service which went into earning it) or even imprisonment, for "speaking with contempt of" the President, the Secretary of Defense, or the Secretary of the Army, Navy, or Air Force.

Compromise

What about the *civilian* experts? How are they kept from criticizing gravedigger programs? No one has ever answered this question quite so aptly as President Eisenhower when he gave his *second* warning in his Farewell Address — *"the power of money."* Here is how he accurately forecast the "buying-up" of research scientists and experts through direct Government employment, plus the expenditure of billions in Government contracts, so they will all speak with one voice — the Administration voice:

"The prospect of domination of the nation's scholars by Federal employment, project allocations, and *the power of money* is ever present — and is gravely to be regarded. . . . In this (technological) revolution, research has become central; it also becomes more formalized, complex, and costly. A steadily increasing share is conducted by, for, or at the direction of the Federal Government. . . . Partly because of the huge costs involved, a Government contract becomes virtually a substitute for intellectual curiosity."

Here is how "the power of money" works in practice. Quite literally hundreds of civilian "experts" in nuclear strategy, science, space, intelligence, international relations, geo-politics, etc., are employed directly by the Government in the highest salary ranges. After observing the operation of the *Fulbright Memorandum* in the Defense Department, and the extension of these same policies of conformity into other Federal agencies,[8] the civilian experts know on which side their bread is buttered, and on which side lie prestige, power, professional and social popularity.

Hundreds more of these "experts" are employed by the numerous so-called "think-tanks," "think-factories," or foundations of "eggheads unlimited" whose chief and often only customer is some agency of the U.S. Government. "The power of money" is the very reason why these "think-tanks" exist. They usually operate under the facade of a "non-profit" charter. Their real purpose is to hire more "scholars" and pay them far more than could be paid if they were directly on the Government payroll. If a scientist or strategist can command more pay than civil service would permit, he can move right in to a "think-tank" and sell the Government a little mimeographed study full of egghead jargon for fantastic prices ranging up to $3,000 per page.[9]

Obviously, "it pays to think" if you can do your thinking at a "think-tank." The Institute for Defense Analyses was established with $500,000 from the Ford Foundation and has about $10 million per year in Pentagon contracts. This is the "think-tank" that sold the *Phoenix Study* to the Government for $78,600 and later produced *Study Fair.* The Pentagon correspondent of the *New York Times* pointed out that the top third of the professional staff at IDA receive larger salaries than Secretary McNamara.[10] The top "think-tank" in the missile and space program, Aerospace, pays its president $76,000 plus $15,000 in "incentive" compensation.[11]

The "think-tanks" generally operate under a curtain of secrecy so that the American people do not know what kind of "thinking" they are doing for us. The Soviets know far more about these mysterious groups and their influence than most American citizens. Here is just one example of the detail of *Soviet* knowledge about U.S. "think-tanks" taken from *Soviet Military Strategy* edited by Marshall V. D. Sokolovskii and 9 other Soviet Generals:

"The RAND Corporation was formed by the U.S. Air Force in 1948 and employs more than 800 prominent scientists. It is charged with the task of determining the types of weapons that satisfy the requirements of contemporary strategy.

"Other similar organizations are the Johns Hopkins University's Operations Research Office (ORO) which does similar work for the Army, the Navy's Operations Evaluation Group at MIT, and the Institute for Defense Analyses, which receives its assignments from the Joint Chiefs of Staff and the Secretary of Defense of the United States."[12]

Thus, by "the power of money," almost all of the civilian experts capable of warning about the gravediggers' programs are effectively compromised because their income comes from Government employment, from corporations with lucrative Government contracts, or from universities receiving heavy Federal aid.

But can't a free press ferret out the news for us? America is fortunate to have some wonderful newsmen who do a superb job. Most, however, are members of the Newspaper Guild, a very, very liberal union, and have advanced in their profession under its ideology. Some are financially compromised by cash payments from the United States Information Agency, other Federal agencies, or tax-exempt foundations made for the purchase of specific articles. A newsman soon learns that if he writes stories friendly to the Administration and the gravediggers, he can augment his income by reselling his articles. Pro-Administration newspapers such as the *New*

York Times, and magazines such as *Life, Time, Newsweek, The Saturday Evening Post, The Saturday Review,* and *Scientific American,* receive Federal subsidies in the form of bulk purchases by the USIA for distribution overseas.[13] The U.S. Arms Control and Disarmament Agency has on its General Advisory Committee two influential newsmen: John Cowles, publisher of the *Minneapolis Star and Tribune* and brother of the publisher of *Look,* and Ralph E. McGill, editor of the *Atlanta Constitution.*[14]

Code Language

Just as parents often converse in front of their children without the little ones understanding the meaning of the conversation, so the gravediggers have learned to speak to each other over the heads of American citizens. The gravediggers use a kind of code language which only the inner circle understands.

Thus, at various national strategy programs and at seminars conducted for the intellectual elite, gravediggers often make speeches which many people hear, but whose esoteric language is beamed over the heads of ordinary participants to other members of the gravedigger elite on the speakers' platform and throughout the influence centers of the nation.

The principal publication used by the gravediggers is *Foreign Affairs,* the quarterly journal of the Council on Foreign Relations. Most of the gravediggers have, at one time or another, written articles in their elite code language for this heavy-paper prestige magazine. Here is where in April

1951 George Kennan, alias "Mr. X," launched his doctrine of "containment" — the U.S. policy which sealed the fate of the Captive Nations. Here is where in April 1964 Roswell Gilpatric announced the gravediggers' plan which will seal the doom of the U.S. by ending our strategic military supremacy. In the July 1965 issue, William C. Foster lays down the Johnson Administration's latest disarmament line: "proliferation" is a greater threat to us than the Soviet nuclear arsenal.

One of the favorite code-language tactics is to pretend to describe plans to be put into effect in the distant future, while describing in careful detail a policy *already* in effect, but kept secret from the American people. For example, the U.S. Arms Control and Disarmament Agency published an official document called *Toward a World Without War*,[15] which describes "Elements of the New U.S. Disarmament Plan" supposedly to be put into effect after we sign a disarmament treaty with the Soviets. Actually it is an accurate description of McNamara's present policy:

> "The U.S. proposal divides the process of disarmament into 3 stages — the first two to be carried out in estimated 3-year periods and the last stage as promptly as possible thereafter. . . . The U.S. plan provides for slashing the nuclear warmaking capacity of nations by 65% during the first 2 stages — estimated 6 years — of the treaty, and eliminating it entirely in the final stage."

The shocking facts are that, under the McNamara policies, *we are already in Stage 2.* In the 5 year he has been in office, McNamara has *already* slashed our nuclear *warmaking* capacity more than 75%.

Then this official booklet, printed by the Government Printing Office, describes the "specific measures" in each of the 3 stages. As explained by Ambassador Arthur Dean, here is what we would do during Stage 1:

> "The United States would have to apply this cut to its B-52 aircraft, to its Titan missiles, to its Atlas missiles, to its submarine-launched Polaris missiles, and to its Hound Dog missiles. . . . In the case of the United States Titan and Atlas missiles, . . . related fixed launching pads would be cut, along with the missiles."

McNamara has scrapped *all* our 1,400 B-47 bombers, and has already started in on the B-52s by eliminating 30 of them. He is not replacing any of the B-52s we lose in Vietnam. He has slashed our Atlas and Titan missiles from 203 to only 54. He has even destroyed all of the launching pads and guidance controls of the 149 big missiles he scrapped.

In Stage 2, "Countries would dismantle or convert to peaceful uses agreed military bases and facilities." McNamara has already dismantled our strategic missile and bomber bases in Turkey, Italy, England and Morocco — plus many in our own country.

These are just samples of the present fulfillment of the plan that the gravediggers *pretend* is for the future. By 1967 we will be moving toward Stage 3. When we complete this stage, having disposed of "all remaining armaments," we will be subject to the "UN Peace Force."

Part of the code language technique used by the gravediggers is their use of obscure words which sound innocuous or like just muddled eggheadism to average Americans, but which are loaded with deadly meaning. For example:

Unilateral-Reciprocal Initiative sounds to the average American like the harmless "you scratch my back and I'll scratch yours." In gravedigger code language it means "Let's not present any more disarmament treaties to the Senate for ratification, because then they are debated and the public finds out what is going on, and the Senate will not approve; instead, let us get rid of our weapons on *our own initiative,* and then, after we have disarmed, we *hope* the Soviets will *reciprocate* and do likewise." This tactic was used by the Kennedy Administration, and is presently being used by the Johnson Administration. It is also called "Interlocking Unilateral Arms Control" — which means, in plain English, disarmament without inspection.[16]

The Pause sounds to the average American like "think before you act." In gravedigger code language it means "we should let the Soviets know in advance that, if they attack, we deliberately do *not* strike back, but *pause,* tell the Soviets what a serious thing they have done, and seek negotiations." Nuclear strategist Herman Kahn said that this "modern" *pause* strategy means that, if the Soviets destroy New York City with 20 megatons,

Lyndon Johnson should *not* retaliate but "stay cool," call up Brezhnev on the "hot line" and ask "was that a mistake?"[17] Common sense tells us that the *pause* could not do otherwise than encourage an aggressor to attack with impunity, especially when he knows in advance that we are going to *pause*.

Measured response does not mean acting only with caution in a tense situation. In gravedigger code language it means "we never hit the Soviets as hard as they hit us." In other words, it is the implementation of the *Fulbright Memorandum* which said:

> "The principal problem of leadership will be, if it is not already, to restrain the desire of the people to hit the Communists with everything we've got, particularly if there are more Cubas and Laos."[18]

Now we have another Laos — in Vietnam. Instead of hitting the Communists with everything we've got, the Administration has given the enemy privileged sanctuaries in Laos, Hanoi and Haiphong.

The measured response has not worked in a small war in Vietnam and there is no reason to think it will work in a big war. Yet, in a nuclear crisis, Herman Kahn explains the measured response like this: if the Soviets bomb out New York City, and we make the mistake of knocking out Moscow, then the intelligent next step is for us *not* to retaliate when the Soviets wipe out Philadelphia![19] *Measured response* means letting the Soviets hit us again and again, but not hitting them in return.

Classification

Congress has traditionally been a watchdog over our nation's defense. The Senate and House Armed Services Committees have always done yeoman's work to make sure the Defense Department has enough billions to guarantee an adequate national defense, and that those billions are well spent.

Three of the gravediggers' curtains of concealment are used particularly to hide their goals from Congressmen, as well as all Americans. The first of these is *Classification.* Whenever Congressmen get too hot on their trail, the gravediggers clamp on the lid of secrecy, scream "classified information," imply that revelation would harm national security — and the bravest Congressmen are silenced. One example was the suppression of how much the Soviets gained by betraying the first nuclear test ban. The Soviets knew exactly, of course; but this information was denied Congress and the American people.

The weapon of "executive privilege," known as the "executive fifth amendment," has also been used and abused by the Johnson Administration to cover bureaucratic mistakes of all kinds. When the questions concern defense, "executive privilege" is a trump card always available to silence Congress, the press and the people.

Complexity

It isn't any accident that matters of defense, missiles and nuclear weapons appear so complicated that most Americans give up all effort to understand them; the gravediggers deliberately planned it that way to camouflage their goal. Complexity is the highly developed technique of making strategic military matters appear so technical and complicated that no one but an "expert" can understand. This tactic is practiced not only on newsmen and the general public, but very successfully on Congressmen, few of whom know nuclear strategy or gravedigger code language.

To prove this for yourself, browse through the 1,556 pages of small print in the *Hearings on Military Posture* before the House Committee on Armed Services, February 2 through March 22, 1965; and, when you finish that, read the 1,261 pages of small print in the *Hearings on Department of Defense Programs* before the Senate Committee on Armed Services, February and March 1965. McNamara's "Statement" alone is 200 large pages, plus tables. Congressmen come from all walks of life, but almost never are engineers or scientists. Furthermore, they have much other work to do, lives to lead, and re-election campaigns to conduct. When the Defense Department is questioned by Congress, McNamara's Whiz Kids "waffle" their answers to bury the big picture in a mass of complicated and irrelevant minutiae. Here is an example of a McNamara waffled statement:

> "I see little merit to the argument that bombers are needed in the Assured Destruction role because our missiles are not dependable. . . . I propose to retain the option to maintain indefinitely bomber units in our Strategic Offensive Forces."[20]

Translated, this means that McNamara will *not* order new improved bombers, such as the B-70, and may not even maintain existing bombers. The argument for bombers is *not* that missiles aren't dependable, but that each B-52 bomber can carry 48 to 120 times the nuclear firepower of our most modern missile, the Minuteman. The B-70 could carry far more — and has more than 3 times the speed. Bombers can be used many times, a missile only once; bombers can be called back after launching; bombers are more flexible as to targeting and force the enemy to defend against a "mix" of delivery systems. Then there is the sobering thought that, if the Soviets continue deploying anti-missiles, our bombers might be needed to come in at low levels to destroy Soviet anti-missile defenses in order to permit our missiles to be effective at all!

Credibility

The ultimate ace-in-the-hole of the gravediggers is that their plot is so incredible to Americans that our people will not believe it. This is their final curtain of concealment on which they depend to protect themselves if the plot is discovered. For example, if you are in a restaurant and overhear a couple of men say they are about to rob the cash register in a local store, you would immediately report it to the police. But if you overhear men say they are about to steal all the gold from Fort Knox, you would not believe it. You dismiss it from your mind as too fantastic to worry about — such things happen only in the far-out fiction of a James Bond thriller.

An example of the technique of incredibility is buried in the official reports of the Senate Armed Services Committee about the controversy over the confirmation of Paul Nitze to be Secretary of the U.S. Navy. In his Asilomar speech in 1960, Nitze made it as plain as gravedigger language can, that he proposed that the United States unilaterally scrap all our most powerful nuclear weapons, give up any attempt to maintain superiority, not even try to make ourselves a "strong second-best," keep only "purely retaliatory weapons" which would be put under NATO and the UN, and rely on the good faith of the Soviets to disarm after we did.

When called before a Senate Committee to explain such fantastic proposals, he was first understood by some of the press to be denying the proposal to put SAC under NATO and the UN.[21] After the Committee put him under oath, he admitted he made the proposals but contended he had not been serious about them! Senator Richard Russell, Chairman of the Committee, recognized that Nitze's explanations could not be reconciled with his Asilomar speech — but he decided to vote for confirmation *"in spite* of his explanations" because he could not believe that such an American would seriously espouse such far-out views.

In other words, when Nitze was caught with his "proposals" showing, he sought refuge behind the curtain of credibility — and it worked. Americans simply cannot believe that other Americans would do things like that to America.

chapter VIII

THE LIE THAT WON
THE ELECTION

All hands agree that the decisive issue of the 1964 presidential election was nuclear war. The majority did not vote for Lyndon Johnson because he is photogenic, but because they were convinced by campaign oratory and television spots that LBJ would keep the peace better than Barry Goldwater. *Newsweek* stated that "an incredible 97% of the Republicans who were going to switch to vote for Lyndon Johnson, were doing so on the nuclear war issue." More than half of Johnson's votes from all other sources were attributed to the nuclear war issue.

One of the principal points in dispute on the issue of nuclear war was Goldwater's charge that:

> "Under our present defense leadership, with its utter disregard for new weapons, our deliverable nuclear capacity may be cut down by 90% in the next decade."[1]

McNamara reacted sharply and had the Pentagon issue a statement which hopelessly complicated the issue for the voters.

Who was right? If the American people had really believed that McNamara is disarming our country by 90%, surely at least 1/3 of those who voted for Johnson on the war issue would have switched their votes. The election would have gone the other way!

After the election, the truth came out. It came from the testimony of one of McNamara's highest officials, whose complete knowledge, authority and integrity cannot be challenged: the Chief of Staff of the U.S. Air Force, General John C. McConnell. Let us compare McNamara's 1964 Official Statement attacking Barry Goldwater with General McConnell's testimony of March 11, 1965.

Defense Department Text, 1964[2]

"Even on its own misleading terms, Senator Goldwater's assertion is false. Even if it were decided that all bombers should be phased out in 1972, and even if megatonnage were the one and only measure of deliverable nuclear capacity — both conditions contrary to fact—the Senator's claim that our strength might be *reduced by 90%* would be false.

"Bomber delivered weapons do not and will not constitute 90% of our strategic force, by any measure, at any time, in the next decade. Senator Goldwater's percentage *is wrong as of today* and still further wrong as applied to the future." (emphasis added)

Air Force Chief of Staff, 1965[3]

"A significant milestone in the history of our strategic forces will occur this coming fiscal year. For the first time there will be more missiles in the force than bombers. This is a result of the phaseout of some B-47 units and the activation of new Minuteman missile units. "However, *the manned bombers still carry some 80%* of the megatonnage currently programmed for delivery by SAC forces and will continue to carry the bulk of these weapons through 1970." (emphasis added)

General McConnell thus confirmed Goldwater's statement that bombers carry most of our megatonnage. The difference between Goldwater's figure of 90% and McConnell's figure of 80% is more than accounted for by the scrapping of bombers that took place between the date of Goldwater's statement and the date of McConnell's statement. McNamara reduced our strategic bombers from 1,100 in 1964[4] to only 680 in 1965.[5] The 420 bombers McNamara scrapped consisted of 30 B-52s (which could carry a 24-megaton bomb each) and 390 B-47s (which could carry a 10-megaton bomb each). Thus, in one year our bomber-deliverable megatonnage was cut 30 x 24 + 390 x 10 = 4,620 megatons, or more than 10% of the U.S. total deliverable megatonnage.

In many authorized interviews and statements, the first of which was featured just a week before the 1964 Presidential election, Secretary of Defense McNamara repeated this boastful theme:

"A comparison of our nuclear forces with Russia's makes our superiority incontestable. . . . In qualitative terms . . . it far exceeds 3 or 4 to 1. . . . There is no indication that they [the Russians] are catching up or planning to catch up with the U.S. in strategic nuclear forces."[6]

This is as false and misleading as Hitler's statement to Prime Minister Chamberlain at Munich on September 23, 1938, "that he had no further territorial ambitions in Europe." McNamara's boast is as dangerous as Gromyko's lie to President Kennedy, uttered in the White House on October 18, 1962 that "Soviet assistance to Cuba . . . was by no means offensive."

Our small missiles do not have the deliverable nuclear capacity of the Soviet giant missiles so we need many bombers. Our 1,270 missiles carry only about 2,300 megatons out of the total of about 40,000 megatons we could deliver at the time of the Cuban crisis. The remainder, more than 90%, was deliverable by the 2,110 Strategic Air Command bombers, plus 600 strategic Naval bombers. The Commander in Chief of SAC, General Thomas S. Power, stated that U.S. military superiority is based on the nuclear firepower of the SAC bombers. The truth of Goldwater's statement that "our deliverable nuclear capacity may be cut down by 90% in the next decade" depends on what happens to our bombers.

Secretary McNamara has reduced our strategic bomber force from 2,110 land-based and 600 carrier-based to only 680, less two which crashed on a Vietnam raid.[7] He ordered the retirement of the last of our 1,400 B-47s although General Power said: "I think the B-47 fleet in the hands of professionals could deliver weapons in the year 2000."[8] McNamara has ignored Congressional appropriations for new strategic bombers and refused to produce the B-70 on the excuse that:

> "Had we decided 2 or 3 years ago to produce the B-70, by the time it came into operation, that is to say in 1967, it would have been obsolete and of little military value."

Clearly, if the new B-70 would be obsolete in 1967, then the much older and slower B-52s and B-58s will be too obsolete by 1967 to be effective.

In other words, McNamara has scrapped 75% of our bomber fleet, representing a loss of potential nuclear firepower of thousands of megatons. In addition, McNamara has cut the bomb loads of the remaining bombers from 24-megaton to 10-megaton bombs, that is, 60%. This means that McNamara has already proved the truth of Goldwater's statement that our deliverable nuclear capacity may be cut 90% in the next decade. Actually, Goldwater was, to use the appropriate word, "conservative" in his estimate. A recent objective survey confirms the more than 90% reduction figure:

"NUCLEAR SHRINKAGE. Massive bomber loads being replaced by relatively small missile warheads. Total deliverable megatonnage in U.S. arsenal will drop from roughly 30,000 to 2,000 in 1970s. U.S. cutting production of fissionable material. Russians reportedly heading in other direction, building 100-megaton weapons — a hundred times greater than Minuteman and Polaris."[9]

Has McNamara built up the rest of our strategic defenses to compensate for what he has done to the bombers? Or is he scrapping them, too?

Drastic Cutback in U.S. Weapons

1. *Destruction of 73% of U.S. Multi-Megaton Missiles.* Since the 1964 election, McNamara has decommissioned 149 of our 203 multi-megaton missiles — the "big guns" of our nuclear arsenal. He has "taken out," more effectively than the enemy ever could, all our multi-megaton Atlas and Titan I missiles, and has even dismantled their launching sites.[10]

2. *No U.S. Super-Missiles.* The United States is not building the super-missiles which are the

decisive weapons of today. The Soviets have built and tested missiles capable of carrying 100-megaton warheads. Of our total proposed missile force for 1970 of 1,710 missiles, 1,656 of them will be in the one-megaton range; our most powerful is the Titan II, estimated at 20 megatons. In their official testimony on August 14, 1963, on the Moscow Test Ban Treaty, the Joint Chiefs of Staff served warning that the Soviets were ahead of us in "high-yield (10's of megatons) technology, in weapons-effect knowledge derived from high-yield nuclear devices, and in the yield/weight ratios of high-yield devices," and that the Moscow Treaty would freeze us in second place.[11] This means that we have guaranteed the Soviets permanent supremacy in warheads capable of destroying our weapons, defenses and population.

Before he was retired by McNamara, Air Force Chief of Staff Curtis LeMay testified that the U.S. should develop a 100-megaton nuclear weapon, and that the Russians already have such a weapon.[12] Since then nothing has been done by McNamara to overcome the U.S.S.R. lead. U.S. one-megaton missiles cannot be equated with the multi-megaton Soviet missiles because the latter have up to 99,000,000 more tons of explosive power. We would need up to 20 times as many long-range missiles as the Soviets just to equal the firepower of the Soviet missiles.

Another way to illustrate the enormous difference in size between our missiles and the Soviet missiles is to recall the Berlin restaurant during World War II which advertised rabbit-horse stew. The advertisement said the stew was 50% rabbit meat and 50% horsemeat. The restaurant did not tell its customers that it was made with one rabbit and one horse! In firepower, our missiles are to the Soviet missiles as one rabbit is to one horse.

McNamara said that as of June 30, 1965, we had 800 Minuteman missiles, 416 Polaris missiles and 54 Titan missiles, for a total of 1,270 long-range missiles; and that the Soviets have only 275 long-range missiles.[13] But McNamara is playing a numbers game because our Minuteman and Polaris average one megaton each, while the Soviet missiles are 10 to 100 megatons each and average about 30 megatons each. Therefore, the total megatonnage of the 275 large Soviet missiles plus their 100+ submarine-fired missiles can be estimated to be up to about 4 times the total power of the 1,270 American missiles.

3. *Retreat from Bases.* A base close to the enemy is one of the most important of all strategic advantages. Five years ago the United States had important missile and bomber bases close to Soviet borders in Europe and Turkey, and the Soviets had none close to us. Today this situation is dramatically reversed. Secretary McNamara closed down all our strategic missile bases close to Russia, and is now closing down our bomber bases in Turkey, Italy, England and North Africa. Meanwhile, in violation of the Monroe Doctrine, the Soviets have built missile and submarine bases in Cuba, only 90 miles off the American coast. The Soviets can also use Cuba for electronic "terminal

guidance" of their ICBMs to score direct hits on U.S. targets.

4. *Destruction of all U.S. Medium-Range Missiles.* McNamara has quietly destroyed all of our medium-range nuclear missiles, including the 105 we had on launching pads in England, Italy and Turkey zeroed in on Soviet targets. His excuse is that these Jupiter and Thor missiles are "obsolete" compared to Polaris which is irrelevant, because they were still highly effective. Furthermore, he refuses to replace them with the Polaris. On August 29, 1964, he stopped all work on a new mobile medium-range missile which the NATO Command declared was essential to the defense of Europe.[14] On May 28, 1965, he restricted deployment of the Davey Crockett, a short-range nuclear missile, in Europe. On July 8, 1965, he ordered the withdrawal of 90 nuclear-armed Mace missiles from Germany, where they "have been aimed at military targets beyond the Iron Curtain on a round-the-clock alert for several years."[15]

5. *Scrapping Good Bombs.* On January 12, 1965, *Newsweek* announced:

> "The U.S. is retiring the biggest weapon in its nuclear arsenal — the 24-megaton bomb. As more missiles go on station, the bomb (designed for the B-52 bomber) has become obsolescent — even though it has never been tested — and is being phased out. 'We knew it would work without ever testing it at full strength,' says one weapons expert."[16]

This is a typical McNamaraism: He claims that our most powerful weapon, with 24 million tons of explosive power, is made obsolete by one-megaton Minuteman missiles!

6. *Production of Nuclear Materials Halved.* Adlai Stevenson told the UN Disarmament Commission on April 26, 1965 that the United States is making large "reductions in the production of plutonium and U-235." Stevenson indicated that the cutbacks announced by President Kennedy in February 1961 and President Johnson in January and April 1965 would exceed 50%.[17]

Abortion of Newly-Developed Weapons

American inventive genius has developed many new strategic weapons. McNamara aborted all of them after the Eisenhower Administration invested millions of dollars in them.

1. *Pluto.* This low altitude, supersonic missile with a hydrogen bomb warhead was called "the most powerful weapon conceived by man." It had a nuclear-powered engine designed to fly it around the world 10 times at 2,000 miles per hour. Because of its speed and low altitude it was invulnerable to existing anti-aircraft or anti-ballistic missile defenses. Abortion of this great weapon by McNamara caused Dr. Edward Teller, "father of our hydrogen bomb," to say:

> "I believe this is the biggest mistake we have made since the years following World War II when we failed to develop the ICBM."[18]

Even the *New York Times* conceded:

> "Pluto did not suffer from technical difficulties or from obsolescence due to other technological developments. There was general agreement,

even among Pentagon critics, of the technical feasibility of guiding the missile."[19]

2. *Skybolt.* This powerful air-to-ground guided nuclear missile would have enabled our bombers to hit enemy targets without flying over enemy soil or within range of their anti-aircraft missiles and guns. It was cancelled by McNamara after British Conservative Party leaders had staked their entire future nuclear defenses on it. In February 1965, McNamara announced a weak substitute of inferior force and short range which he called the SRAM (Short Range Attack Missile), but which is popularly referred to as the "SHAM."

3. *B-70 Bomber.* This is the greatest large airplane ever built. Ten years ago the Eisenhower Administration planned that the B-70 would replace the B-52 in 1965. Its speed is 3 times greater, and it has set new records for supersonic flight. The U.S. spent $1.5 billion, 10 years work, and the efforts of 3,000 engineers — and the B-70 was proved a brilliant success.[20]

4. *Mobile Nuclear Missiles.* "A highly effective strategy for improving survivability is mobility." Yet McNamara cancelled the tested plan to equip each of 60 trains with "5 [Minuteman] missiles in fast-erecting launchers, all necessary communication, electronic and power equipment, as well as living quarters for the crew," and to similarly equip ships.[21] McNamara also cancelled the program for mobile, Medium-range nuclear missiles for NATO, which would deter a Soviet attack.

5. *Additional Nuclear-Powered Aircraft Car-*

riers. These cost no more than air bases in foreign countries, have the advantage of not being a fixed target for enemy missiles, and can cruise indefinitely. Our first and only nuclear-powered carrier, the Enterprise, is a big success. But McNamara and our new Secretary of the Air Force, Harold Brown, killed the plan to construct more as planned by the Eisenhower Administration.

6. *Dynasoar.* This orbital spacecraft capable of performing various military missions, and, upon re-entry, of gliding under its pilot's control to land on airfields (instead of merely splashing down in the ocean, like all other American space vehicles) was cancelled by McNamara.

Refusal to Develop New Weapons

Napoleon went to his Waterloo because he rejected Robert Fulton's offer to build for him the world's first steamboat — the one weapon that could have defeated the wind-driven British Navy. Germany lost World War I because Hindenberg rejected the offer of the American Holt Tractor Company to build a revolutionary new weapon made by putting armorplate and machine guns on a tractor; 3 years later, the Allies seized the idea and made the *tank* the decisive weapon. Hitler lost on sea and in air because the Nazis failed to grasp the military significance of radar, jet propulsion and atomic power.

Likewise, McNamara and other gravediggers in the Pentagon have vetoed plans to develop the vital weapons of the future. Hanson Baldwin, military editor of the *New York Times*, charges:

". . . today the main stumbling blocks to the

rapid development of military space projects are Secretary McNamara and his Director of Defense Research and Engineering, Dr. Harold Brown, who in his new political role in the Pentagon has become a remarkably unadventurous scientist."[22]

Here is a partial list of weapons and defense systems which McNamara and Brown have failed to research, develop, procure, or deploy.

1. *Orbital Bombs* are nuclear weapons which can be placed in orbit and then, upon radio signal, deliver a vertical nuclear attack. Brezhnev has announced that the U.S.S.R. now has enough "intercontinental and orbital rockets so that once and forever we can put an end to any aggressor or any group of aggressors."[23]

2. *Gigaton Bombs* are terrifying weapons in the thousand-megaton range. A Soviet rocket capable of orbiting the 26,500-pound-payload Proton 1 is capable of delivering a cluster of 100-megaton warheads. Informed Americans believe that the Soviets have such weapons.[24]

3. *Neutron Bombs.* Development has been long demanded by concerned patriots such as Congressman Craig Hosmer, Chairman of the Weapons Subcommittee of the Joint Committee on Atomic Energy, who said the neutron bomb could be used "to stem aggressors without destroying the lives of the friendly population, without causing wholesale damage to cities and farmlands." Although prominent scientists such as Dr. Freeman J. Dyson have said the neutron bomb is

feasible, McNamara and Harold Brown refuse to develop it.[25]

4. *Anti-Missile and Anti-Satellite Defenses.* In football the defense is almost as important as the offense, but in war it may be far more important. The failure of McNamara and Harold Brown to produce and deploy any anti-missile defense is culpable negligence because it endangers 195 million American lives. A landlord who permits a fire trap is criminally responsible. McNamara is permitting a nuclear fire death trap for, in his own figures, 71 million Americans. Dr. Edward Teller, our greatest nuclear weapons designer, warned on July 26, 1965:

> "The United States should, without delay, put the greatest possible stress on the defensive against missiles. At present we are spending on this important enterprise less than one percent of our military budget."

Lt. General Arthur G. Trudeau, former Army Chief of Research and Development, said:

> "With no defense against missiles or satellites worthy of the name, we stand forth today as the world's greatest nuclear nudist colony."[26]

5. *Nuclear Shelters.* Had the U.S. fleet at Pearl Harbor not been "sitting ducks," there probably would never have been a surprise attack against it. If McNamara permitted the strong anti-missiles, anti-satellite and shelter defenses of which we are capable, we would not be in our present danger of a surprise attack.

McNamara has failed to produce a single new strategic weapon in 5 years. The proof is in the budget. McNamara's budget for "Strategic Offensive and Strategic Defensive Forces" shrunk $2 billion for fiscal year 1963-64, $4 billion or 37% for 1964-65, and $5 billion or 45% for 1965-66.[27] And even these diminishing amounts are all expended for strategic weapons systems developed in the Eisenhower Administrations.

For the first couple of years, the McNamara cutbacks in our defense were not very apparent. But just as the law of gravity says that falling bodies accelerate in speed, so the policy of reducing our military strength has been accelerating until, after 5 years, it is moving at tremendous momentum. McNamara's cutbacks and cancellations, plus his failure to build the new weapons of the future, are carrying out the Nitze-Gilpatric proposals to make America a poor second in the strategic arms race. All events since November 1964 have vindicated the 27 million Americans who voted for *real* military strength instead of a hoax.

Near-Disaster in Vietnam

With so much evidence that McNamara's policies are exposing the United States to destruction by a nuclear holocaust striking us from space — how is he doing in protecting America from encirclement and ultimate defeat through a series of "little wars" staged by the Communists? For more than 5 years, the Kennedy and Johnson Administrations have been claiming a successful build-up of "vastly superior" *conventional* military strength to provide a "flexible response." Vietnam gave us our first real chance to evaluate Mc-

Namara's claims on the basis of actual experience. What are the facts?

On May 26, 1964 Secretary McNamara referred to reports of shortages and obsolete equipment in Vietnam as "absolutely without foundation." Throughout the 1964 campaign and as late as an authorized interview in April 1965, McNamara said:

> "News stories recently indicated shortages of equipment, or distribution to Vietnam of obsolete equipment. There was no basis for them whatsoever."[28]

After the 1964 election, a Senate Armed Services Subcommittee spent months digging out the truth. Its report, issued in August 1965, was an inch thick. It concluded that shortages did in fact exist. At this point, the curtain of classification was invoked to keep the American people from discovering specific evidence of how dangerously short we were in materiel needed by our fighting men in Vietnam. The Subcommittee's report was so heavily censored that parts of it looked like this:

> "Senator Stennis: "I want to make an observation as a member of the Subcommittee about the matter of (deleted). It appears that (deleted). (Deleted) This is serious (deleted)."[29]

Fortunately, several newspapers and newsmagazines were able to break through the curtain of classification and produce evidence of the falsity of McNamara's categorical denial of *any* shortages in Vietnam. The Senate investigation revealed shortages and deficiencies totaling $12 billion.[30] In *communications* there were shortages of equipment from the walkie-talkies for squad leaders all the way to the highly complex equipment for division headquarters. There were shortages in spotting systems for mortars, warning systems for the protection of our men against hostile aircraft, and guidance and control equipment to give fast, low-flying bombers the pinpoint accuracy they need to hit their targets and save our own men. In *transportation,* our wealthy nation, which turns out millions of new luxury automobiles every year, offered its soldiers and fighting Marines mostly obsolete equipment — trucks and troop carriers of Korean War and even World War II vintage. Even helicopters were in short supply. In *ordnance,* there were shocking shortages of ammunition for .30 and .50 cal. machine guns, for 20 mm. anti-tank guns, and even for M-14 rifles![31] In August 1965 *U.S. News & World Report* devoted 3 pages to reporting how shortages were hampering our combat troops in Vietnam, summarizing with a bold-face heading:

"SHORTAGES OF SUPPLIES ARE SEEN EVERYWHERE, COVER A WIDE RANGE, G-I'S, READY FOR ACTION, ARE RESORTING TO MAKESHIFT GEAR."[32]

Other news accounts revealed that some of the largest U.S. groups were fighting in tennis shoes in areas where lack of proper footwear could literally cause death. Although McNamara had claimed vast improvements in air and sea lift, the UPI reported:

"The Commander of the Army's new mobile air

division vetoed plans to ship his helicopter
crews to Vietnam in the hold of a rusty 'mothball
fleet' aircraft carrier. Major General Harry
Kinnary . . . ruled that conditions aboard were
substandard and not fit for his airmen."[33]

Why were there shortages in Vietnam? Here is
one never-before-revealed example of what Mc-
Namara has done. The St. Louis Ordnance Plant
was the largest producer of .30 and .50 caliber
ammunition during World War II. It turned out
6,718,230,796 cartridges and bullets and had a
peak employment of 42,000 people. In 1946 the
plant was dismantled, the equipment sold or
scrapped, and the buildings turned into a Government records center. When the Korean War came
along, the plant was re-equipped and reactivated
— of course, at a far higher cost.

After the Korean War, the Eisenhower Defense
Department did not make the same mistake the
Truman Administration made in 1946. In 1955
the entire plant was put on a "lay-away" basis.
A beautiful job was done of preparing the equipment to keep it in perfect condition; all the machinery was greased and carefully covered. Like
this, the plant would have remained in excellent
condition for 20 years, ready to produce on a day's
notice. The plant remained like this from 1955
through 1960.

Then came McNamara. In one of the gigantic
giveaways of all time, McNamara *gave* the entire
ammunition plant to India. A special appropria-
tion covered the expensive job of crating all the
machinery and moving it to New Orleans. Then

it was shipped to India and in 1963 installed on a site 155 miles west of New Delhi. There the plant began producing ammunition in the summer of 1965, just in time for the India-Pakistan war. The result is that this great plant *twice* paid for by the U.S. taxpayers — was producing ammunition to kill our Pakistani friends instead of to save our own men in Vietnam. This is just one example of what has happened in the field of *conventional* weapons on which McNamara has concentrated.[34]

McNamara's Numbers Game

All through the 1964 political campaign, in press conferences, in magazine articles and to the Democratic Party Platform Committee, and even in 1965, McNamara made repeated claims of vast increases in our conventional strength. The figures he most often used were:

"A 45% increase in the number of combat-ready Army divisions. A 44% increase in the number of tactical fighter squadrons. A 75% increase in air-lift capability. An 800% increase in the Department of Defense Special Forces trained for counter insurgency."[35]

These figures were supposed to mean that we have "enough" military strength to meet any Communist threat. But if we had just *one* man in counter-insurgency forces, an 800% increase would mean we now have only 8 men; if 100, then 800. What did McNamara mean? Apparently he did not intend for us to know.

It is amazing how McNamara has gotten away, ever since 1962, with the claim of "a 45% increase in the number of combat-ready Army divisions."

This conveys to the average American an Army increase to nearly half-again its previous number of fighting men. At the end of the Eisenhower Administration, the Army had 14 divisions; so the increase in the number of divisions would be understood to be 6, bringing the total up to 20. The Army's pre-McNamara strength was 900,000 men; so the increase expected would be about 400,000 men. The increase we got was only 63,273 or 7%.

The slick arithmetic on divisions is even more tricky. Under Eisenhower, 3 of the 14 divisions were considered to be "in training." This gave McNamara the chance to subtract 3 from the total of 14, leaving 11. Based on this, a 45% increase in the number of Army divisions would be only 5 additional divisions. McNamara produced 3 divisions by the simple expedient of giving some new combat equipment (ordered during the Eisenhower Administration but still in the process of delivery) to the 3 divisions previously considered "in training"; then McNamara labelled them "combat-ready." McNamara then ordered a re-division of manpower and simply created 2 new divisions out of what had already existed.

All of the new total of 16 divisions were then classified as "combat-ready." But there was no more substance than we had under the Eisenhower Administration. This took only a stroke of the McNamara pen — and who could challenge his claim of a 45% increase in combat divisions? But history stepped in to expose McNamara's claims. When Army divisions were urgently needed in

Vietnam in the early summer of 1965, they proved to be so *un-*"combat-ready" that it would take months to move them to the combat zone — so the Marines had to be sent in.

Another of McNamara's projects was to "merge" the Army Reserve into the National Guard and reduce their combined strength from 700,000 to 550,000. At a time when even an amateur could see that there might be urgent need for calling up the Reserves in a hurry, McNamara proposed to discharge 150,000 trained men whose patriotism and will to serve had been proved.

This McNamara measure was a ruthless blow to the morale of the entire Reserve. For some 10 to 20 years, these men had been giving their time to Reserve training. When McNamara announced that the Reserve was not worthwhile, that to abolish it would "permit improved readiness of National Guard Divisions," this was like telling our Reserves: "All your time and your country's money spent on your training was wasted." This was too much for Congress to stomach. Congress wrote into a defense appropriations bill a prohibition of any such merger before June 30, 1966.[36]

Within a few weeks, however, it became apparent that McNamara was evading this prohibition by Congress, just as he had ignored earlier Congressional mandates to produce a new bomber and to develop space weapons. His first move to get around the law against "merger" of Reserve Units was to claim that he was now "dissolving" them. But the result was the same—he "killed" 751 Army Reserve Units containing 55,000 men.

Vietnam was the "testing ground" for Mc-Namara's judgment of how much is "enough" to meet a conventional challenge "with incontestable superiority." He flunked the test against a 30th-rate power — half of a poor, unindustrialized, underdeveloped country. McNamara was so far short of "enough" to meet such a challenge that we were very close to losing the war in the summer of 1965. Even to attain a stalemate, it was decided to add another 300,000 men to the U.S. Armed Services.

Ever since he took office, McNamara supposedly has been concentrating on "conventional" forces and weapons. If McNamara can be so dangerously wrong about preparedness for little wars, how can he meet and turn back the Soviet threat of a hydrogen holocaust? If you had a fire chief who couldn't put out little fires, would you trust him to put out a big one? In Vietnam we could afford a year to redress the McNamara mistakes. Against Soviet multi-megaton missiles, we would not have a year, not a month, not a day — perhaps only a half hour. Against a gigaton strike from space, we could expect no warning at all. If our *strategic* nuclear power is not sufficient *to deter* the Soviets from striking, America will be destroyed!

chapter IX

SAVING FACE IN SPACE

Suppose this book had gone to press earlier. After detailing the *cut*-back in strategic bombers and missiles to 1/10 of our former strength, the second part would show that the secret plan of the gravediggers calls for a *hold*-back in space weapons to *zero*. The evidence would show that the secret plan will not permit us to develop any defense against Soviet space weapons, will not allow us to produce interceptors to shoot them down from space, nor anti-orbital bomb systems to shoot them down from earth.

No American wants to believe such things. There would have been great relief, therefore, on August 25, 1965 when President Johnson announced the Manned Orbiting Laboratories program. This feeling would have grown to elation and patriotic pride upon reading news stories about how MOL will speed us ahead in the space race. Even the publications which do not go all the way with LBJ joined the chorus of praise in the belief that Johnson had swung to the "hard" line and committed America to a race for military supremacy in space.

If this were true, it would indeed be the greatest strategic decision since World War II. It would assure peace and freedom to all living Americans, their children and grandchildren. Is the MOL program really a commitment to a race for military supremacy in space? Or did it merely mean that the Masters of Managed News had been warned by their computers that the many articles which had appeared in news media contrasting the Soviet concentration on *military* programs in space with the *pacifist* U.S. attitude were beginning to have their effect? The American people, knowing that we can now take a walk in space, were demanding to know *where we are going in space.* How can we identify the true character of the MOL decision? The clues must be sought, the evidence weighed.

The first clue is provided by the answer to the question, what will MOL do? If it won't worry the Soviets or challenge their strategic supremacy, it's bound to be a sop. It will be a better sop, of course, if it does nothing -- but at the same time can be the basis for much high-sounding talk about all sorts of science-fiction space armament. If, on the other hand, it will do something in a military way to counter Soviet space-weapon threats, if it will thwart their seizing control of "inner space" — then, and only then, will it be evidence that the United States has finally decided to enter the space race in order to defend America.

The wish is often father of the thought. The press was so carried away by its hope that many pages were filled with enthusiastic predictions unsupported by any evidence. Coming down to earth, here is Secretary McNamara's own explanation of the primary and *only* "military objectives" of the MOL program:

"(1) Development of technology contributing to improved military capability for manned or unmanned operations. This *may* include *intermediate* steps toward operational systems.

"(2) Development and demonstration of manned assembly and servicing in orbit of large structures with potential military applications. This will interact strongly with the preceding objectives.

"(3) Other manned military space experimentation."[1] (emphasis added)

There is the answer to the big question: MOL can do nothing in the way of operational military missions other than can already be done by unmanned U.S. satellites and earlier model manned vehicles such as Gemini. MOL is purely experimental, as its name "Laboratory" implies. MOL cannot carry out inspection and possible destruction of hostile satellites — unless, by pure chance of one in several billion, it should collide with one. MOL cannot even rendezvous with our own space vehicles. MOL cannot alter its orbital path for interception of hostile vehicles, nor does it even have a planned weapons system for destroying them.

The only operational military mission MOL could perform would be reconnaissance; and the wonderful cameras of unmanned satellites can "see" far more. Nor is MOL a "transitional stage" between our present orbital vehicles and future space weapons. The most that can be claimed for it is that it "may" include the development of technology leading to "intermediate" steps toward operational systems.

Do these negative evaluations mean MOL is worthless? By no means. It is highly desirable, even essential. It is so good that it was stalled in the Defense Department for more than a year. As late as February 1965, McNamara was still holding it in the "option" state.[2] In Pentagon language, this means that actual development of a program is being blocked, but the "stall" is conducted in a sophisticated manner so that critics cannot contend that McNamara has actually "killed" the program.

What this means is that MOL, by itself, is far too little and too late to compete with the Soviets for military control over the belt of "inner space" which in turn can control the world. Even the first *unmanned* MOLs are not scheduled for trial until 1968 — and experience tells us to expect much "slippage" in U.S. space programs.

The experiments MOL would conduct could not produce any concrete proposals for "intermediate steps" toward space weapons or even space defense systems for another couple of years. When the "intermediate steps" go into development, another 5 years could be expended. Then, based on actual experience, another 5 to 10 years would be required for development of space weapons or defense systems.

How does MOL stack up against Soviet space vehicles? MOL will carry two men in its crew. Soviet space accomplishments are dramatic:

"Voskhod spaceship, already operational, can be

turned into space platform for 3 to 5 man crews. Proton I, latest Soviet space vehicle, weighs 13½ tons, is ready to orbit 6 to 8 man crews, carry vast amounts of military equipment."[3]

These Soviet space ships are operational now! The most optimistic prediction for actual manned MOL flights is the *end* of 1968 — 3-1/2 years from the time that President Johnson pulled it out of McNamara's "option" limbo and after the Soviets orbited Proton 1. This verifies the long held, almost never publicized, conclusion that *the Soviets are more than 5 years ahead of us in military payloads for space.*

The Gilpatric Space Policy

Even if MOL does not amount to much in itself, even if it will leave us far behind the Soviets, does it nevertheless signal adoption by the Administration of a new "hard" U.S. strategy for space? U.S. policy was revealed in 1962 in a speech by the then Deputy Secretary of Defense, Roswell Gilpatric:

"An arms race in space will not contribute to our security. I can think of no greater stimulus for a Soviet thermonuclear arms effort in space than a U.S. commitment to such an effort. This we will not do."

Sophisticated, but positive. This is an absolute declaration that the Administration will not compete in an arms race in space. This policy includes all the prime ingredients of the gravediggers' doctrines: sophistry — it's safer to be weak than to be strong; defeatism — we can't win an arms race against the Soviets; and trust the Communists — if we don't provoke them, they won't attack.

This Gilpatric version of U.S. military space policy has been in effect at least since October 17, 1963, when we were bound by the U.S.-sponsored (Pugwash-initiated) United Nations resolution against orbiting weapons of mass destruction. Like the first nuclear test ban, it has absolutely no provision for inspection or enforcement.

Furthermore, the UN "agreement" does *not* prohibit developing and producing and even orbiting space ships *capable* of carrying warheads which could accomplish mass destruction. This gives the Soviets two ways to cheat: first, without violating the letter of the UN resolution, they can develop and produce an entire fleet of orbital bombers, but not orbit them until shortly before their strike. This would give the Soviets a lead-time advantage over us of at least 5 years. The Soviets have repeatedly claimed they have produced such orbital bombers.[4] The second way is by out-and-out cheating, through taking advantage of the no-inspection requirement. How can we tell what is really in Proton I's orbiting 26,500 pounds?

There is great evidence that President Johnson's August 25, 1965 MOL decision is wholly in line with the Gilpatric declaration of a firm commitment *against* entering a military space race with the Soviets. In fact, President Johnson expressly reaffirmed that policy in these words:

> "We intend to live up to our agreement not to orbit weapons of mass destruction."[5]

Unfortunately, we are also holding to the self-imposed restriction not found in the letter of the UN Resolution, and which the Soviets openly declare they are not abiding by, of not developing and producing orbital bombers.

The then Director of Research and Engineering of the Defense Department, now Secretary of the Air Force, Dr. Harold Brown, testified in 1964 that "not more than a couple of hundred thousand dollars" a year is being spent on orbital bombardment research, with "not more than 3 or 4 people . . . studying this question." He gave two reasons: "first, it is not a very good idea," and "second, there is now a UN Resolution which we subscribe to and the Soviets have subscribed to. . . ."[6] Against our couple of hundred thousand dollars, the Soviets may be investing many billions on orbital bomber projects.

Johnson's decision to adopt the MOL program did not change or repudiate the long-standing Gilpatric policy of refusing to engage in a military space race with Russia — because MOL is neither a weapons system in itself, or capable of becoming one, or even capable of leading directly to development of any space weapons systems. Unless and until it becomes evident that the Administration is devoting substantial resources to research and development of actual space weapons systems, it is obvious that the Gilpatric policy is still being strictly enforced.

As always in the U.S. space program, the big money and the huge national effort go to prestige projects. Only the crumbs are left for military space programs which could insure our survival and our freedom, as well as peace on earth. MOL has not been given priority over any part of the Moon project, nor has it even been put on an equal basis with such non-vital programs.

To sum up, our race in space is solely to save face. It is *not* to defend America from an attack which could destroy us. The moondoggle is a diversion — it looks strong to Americans, but the Soviets, who are *not* racing to the moon,[7] know there is no military value in that trip.

Stacked in space, stockpiled in the sky — the Soviets now have more than 85 *known* Cosmos satellites, with *unknown* payloads.[8] How many of the Cosmos are orbital bombers, armed as General Power warned they could be, with "multimegaton nuclear weapons which could be released upon radio command from Russia"?[9]

No one on our side knows the answer. We do have a clue — from high authority on their side: from First Party Secretary Leonid Brezhnev, former czar of the Soviet space program, co-conspirator in the plot to destroy the United States from Cuba. In mid-summer 1965, published boasts in U.S. papers of McNamara's small-warheaded U.S. missiles had put the Minuteman number at 800, and had downgraded Soviet multi-megaton missiles to 270-300. The Kremlin felt it could afford a little derisive understatement in reply:

> " 'We hate to boast, and we do not want to threaten anyone,' Brezhnev confided delicately to the graduates of the Soviet Military Academies in Moscow. 'However, it is necessary to note that

the figures and calculations quoted in the West about *rocket* and nuclear power of the Soviet Union do no credit at all to the intelligence services of imperialist states.' "[10] (emphasis added)

Pentagon planners are constantly writing up "scenarios" for "war games" so they can play-act-out visions of future wars. What would a scenario of a strike from space be like? At evening rush hour on the east coast, 3 gigaton orbital bombs would be fired by radio command with zero warning — each covering 1/3 of our nation. The Proton I fleet would be de-orbited and exploded over major population centers and Minuteman missile areas. All communication and command facilities would be hopelessly damaged, including our "Looking Glass" Command on continuous airborne alert. Even if there were any U.S. official left alive with authority and the code to command our Polaris submarines to retaliate, how could he communicate? Then the attack would continue immediately with missiles from Soviet submarines, from Cuba, and over the South Pole. Within 15 minutes, the Cosmos series of orbital bombs would be de-orbited and fired, plus 100-megaton missiles fired from Siberia. Soviet bombers would arrive soon after to mop up any targets still undestroyed.

Secretary McNamara estimated 149 mega-deaths from a Soviet missile attack — and he did not figure space weapons or bomber mop-up. The stark fact is — if the Soviets play this scenario for real — the American people would be assassinated as a whole. The Soviets would then hold the rest of the world in ruthless slavery.

chapter X

PEACE OF THE KNAVE

What is the shocking secret the gravediggers have hidden so successfully behind 6 curtains of concealment? Why do they slant their managed news to convince Americans we are 3 or 4 times stronger than the Soviet Union and winning the race to the moon — when, in fact, they are scrapping U.S. military might and defaulting us in the race for military control of space?

To find the only solution which explains all the gravediggers' actions, we must get "inside" their minds to find out how they think. Only then can we translate their super-sophisticated language into plain English. To "dig" the gravediggers, we must recognize their 3 characteristics: they have no real faith in the American people, in the U.S. Constitution, or in God. They complain because the American people sometimes veto the judgments of public officials.[1] They believe our U.S. Constitution is outmoded and unduly restrains the Executive;[2] even worse, its safeguards stand in the way of disarmament treaties with the Soviets.[3] God, if He exists at all, is a "neutralist" in the war being waged by the Communist slavemasters against freedom and religion.

George S. Kennan, the chief theoretician of the gravediggers and prime architect of U.S. policy relating to Communism, does not hesitate to claim to read God's mind. After declaring that the differences between democracy and authoritarianism are merely "relative and do not present clearcut issues," after comparing the two forms so as to downgrade our side and upgrade the Communist side, he warns us

> "We must concede the possibility that there might be some areas involved in this cold war which a Divine Power could contemplate only with a sense of pity and disgust for both parties, and others in which he might even consider us wrong."[4]

The gravediggers are passionately opposed to defending the 195 million American citizens against a Soviet-launched nuclear holocaust by a policy of deterrence based on *even the threat* of nuclear retaliation. Secretary of the Navy Paul Nitze characterized retaliation as an "irrational" act.[5] George Kennan has repeatedly said that we have no justification for a policy of retaliation against a nuclear strike against us. He claims

> "It will be said to me: This means defeat. To this I can only reply: I am skeptical of the meaning of 'victory' and defeat in their relation to modern war between great countries."[6]

In his latest book, he concludes that our greatest obligation to our children is to preserve the "physical intactness of our environment," and we can leave to them "the more traditional problems of international life." The implication is clear: if we have a choice between selling our children into Communist slavery or defending their freedom by means which might impair the "physical intactness of our environment," then we should accept the sell-out.

As the gravediggers see it, the big Problem is this: A Soviet surprise strike against America would result in 149 million deaths, according to McNamara's estimates — *including* nearly all the gravediggers, because they live and work in prime target areas. What are the alternative solutions?

1. *Increased Deterrence.* We can attempt to deter the Soviet strike by U.S. nuclear superiority. This would require a vast buildup in the numbers and explosive power of our long-range missiles and bombers, together with crash efforts to protect our strategic weapons and population by anti-missile systems. Our objective would be to convince the Soviets that they could not profit by striking us, and we would guarantee them a catastrophic loss if they did strike. Knowing how the gravediggers think, this solution would be repugnant to their credo. They are all defeatists, convinced that the American system cannot compete with the Soviets. Every policy of McNamara and every paper written by the gravediggers gives testimony that they have rejected this solution.

2. *A Defensive-Disarming Strike.* The second possible solution to the threatened Soviet strike is to wait until the strike is imminent. At that point, morality permits, and the first rule of self-preservation and international law requires that, if you have strategic weapons able to disarm the enemy of the weapons he is about to launch at you, you fire at him just in the nick of time. A defensive-

disarming strike is an act of self-defense to disarm the enemy in the last inch of time — just like the sheriff who beats the bad guy to the draw.

The fact that McNamara has scrapped 3/4 of our multi-megaton missiles (149 out of 203) plus the 105 medium-range missiles we had in Turkey, Italy and England, is a sure giveaway that the gravediggers have rejected the possibility of a defensive-disarming strike at the last minute. Most of them even oppose striking back after the Soviets have hit us. These most effective weapons are now gone. Our Minutemen and Polaris by themselves, if used in a disarming strike, would guarantee us nothing but national suicide because of the Soviet super-weapons they could *not* destroy.

Preemptive Surrender

3. *Preemptive Surrender.* This is a request to the enemy, after he has decided to attack, to be allowed to surrender instead of being subjected to the attack. Instead of making the enemy attack *impossible* by a defensive-disarming strike, preemptive surrender is designed to make the threatened attack *unnecessary*. The aggressor gets everything he wants without actually making the attack. Preemptive surrender would work this way: If, after we discovered the Soviet strategic missiles in Cuba in 1962, the President had sent Khrushchev a message saying: "Don't fire — we surrender" — that would have been preemptive surrender. Preemptive surrender can also be camouflaged by phrasing it in political rather

than military terms; then we would call it "preemptive accommodation."

If we put ourselves in the place of the gravediggers, and think as their ideology compels them, this is the only solution that fits. It meets the insistent demand of George Kennan, voiced as far back as 1959, that we "wean ourselves from this fateful and pernicious principle of first use."[7] It is not an "irrational act" as the Nitze Asilomar speech describes retaliation against our enemies.

The evidence is overwhelming that the gravediggers have adopted a plan to reduce U.S. strategic power so drastically by unilateral disarmament that we would have no alternative to national suicide other than a preemptive surrender. The psychology of the gravediggers, the documentary evidence of their speeches and reports, and the actual defense policies of the McNamara-Nitze-Gilpatric-Brown axis all force us to the same conclusion.

Why should this be hard to believe when the Europeans, especially those in the NATO countries, have clearly accepted this same policy if the American deterrent fails to protect them? Nuclear strategist Herman Kahn reports that surrender plans

> "are the implicit and sometimes explicit tactics of the Europeans. . . . Very few Europeans believe that a nation can justifiably commit suicide or initiate actions which would lead to its total extinction, or even watch passively if events are occurring which have a high probability of leading to such a result."[8]

In another study, Dr. Kahn put it this way:

"This, then, is my observation. The basic central war policy in Europe is what we at Hudson call 'preemptive surrender' or 'preemptive accommodation.' "9

If the Europeans would accept a policy of preemptive surrender for their own nations, why not the gravediggers?

The mere suggestion of the preemptive surrender of the United States is so appalling to the average American that emotionally he cannot believe it. Could Americans in positions of tremendous trust and responsibility, really do such a thing as to disarm us deliberately so that, under threat of a Soviet strike from space, we would have no alternative to a preemptive surrender? The gravediggers are men who enjoy all the material comforts of the American private-enterprise system. They are men with "status" and power in the political, intellectual, academic, business and scientific communities. They have more to lose than anyone else. How could they trade in the good life they now have for surrender to a Communist world? *Why?*

The answer is frighteningly simple. The gravediggers are just human beings who don't think anything is worth dying for; they act solely from the fundamental motive of self-preservation. Scientific evidence has convinced them that the Soviets will inevitably win the arms race and strike first. Therefore, since the Soviets are going to win anyway, it is better to make the best deal we can with the Soviets and let them win without a nuclear holocaust. The gravediggers know they have a lot to lose, but they know they won't be any better off as a rich cinder than a poor cinder; so they think they would rather be Red than dead. They are throwing away our third choice to stay strong and thus remain free and alive.

The gravediggers know that, if Americans have a fighting chance to defend ourselves, we will fight rather than surrender. This is the tradition of a nation which has never known defeat. The gravediggers believe that the Soviets will surely win because they are stronger and, if we fight, America will be destroyed including the gravediggers. So the gravediggers have made the decision for us, and *they plan to keep it secret until it is too late to retrace our steps.* The gravediggers are convinced that the only way to avoid nuclear destruction is to make sure that we are so completely disarmed that even the military would not resist because they would know it would be suicide to try.

The gravediggers are not Communists. Communists are motivated by their dedication to an ideal, mistaken though it is. The gravediggers are not dedicated to anything except saving their own skins. The gravediggers sincerely think they are doing the best thing for America because they believe that we, too, should rather be Red than dead. They think we should be grateful to them for saving our lives by disarming us. They think this is the best way to end the possibility of mutual nuclear annihilation. They think world peace can be secured if the U.S. abandons the arms race and lets the Soviets win. The timing of their strategy is governed by the timetable of the Soviet strike from space. The gravediggers plan that the strike will be preempted just in time.

Don't the gravediggers know that, after the Communists take over a country, they send the leaders of a conquered nation to mass graves? No, they don't. The gravediggers may fare quite well after surrender. The gravedigger scientists may be treated as the German scientists were treated after they were captured by the Russians — which was very well indeed. The German scientists had a talent the Soviets coveted, so they were allowed to live in comfort and ease, enjoy a good income, respect and status in their community — as long as they put forth their best efforts to make the U.S.S.R. supreme in rockets to carry nuclear weapons.

The Soviets may feel so indebted to the gravediggers who are not scientists that they will fare well as Commissars under their new masters. It might be thought that the Kremlin would need reliable natives to administer an occupied America and that those who had demonstrated their helpfulness to the Kremlin would be indispensable.

When the gravediggers write in their egghead treatises about "convergence" or "merger" or "unification" of the U.S. and the U.S.S.R., they are really talking about the condition which will exist after the preemptive surrender of America. They hope that, in time, the Soviets will grow more like us, and that, although the big decisions will be made in the Kremlin, we can enjoy much of our present good life.

Let us examine the peroration of a 1965 gravedigger speech by George Kennan:

> "I . . . plea for something resembling a new act of faith in the ultimate humanity and sobriety of the people on the other side. . . . In the predication of only the worst motives on the adversary's part there lies today no hope at all. . . . Our sole hope lies in the possibility that the adversary, too, has learned something from the sterility of past conflict; . . . that some reliance can be placed, in the adjustment of mutual differences, on his readiness to abstain, voluntarily and in self-interest, from the wildest and most senseless acts of physical destruction. If this possibility fails us, we have little to fall back on."[10]

Now let's translate this remarkable paragraph from its gravedigger code language. On the solemn occasion of this address in New York before a distinguished audience of 2,000 people, Kennan pleads for an act of faith — in what? Not in God, not in our country, not in the ideals that made America great — but for an act of faith in the "humanity" of the Communists. He wants Americans to forget Katyn Forest, forget the slave labor camps, forget the genocide of the Captive Nations, forget the butchery of Budapest, forget the American soldiers who were tortured and murdered in Korea, and believe that Communists *are* humane.

Kennan then reveals the basic defeatism of all gravediggers. He says we have "no hope at all" if we believe the Communists have the "worst motives." Yet the objective evidence of history certainly indicates they do have the worst motives.

Finally, Kennan concludes that "our sole hope" lies in the willingness of the Soviets "to abstain, voluntarily" from a nuclear attack on us; if that fails, *there is no other hope.* In other words, there is *no* hope from the military strength of the United States. There is *no* hope from McNamara's Minutemen, or from his promise that we are 4 times stronger than the Soviets.

Do the American people want to have our future and the future of our children rest *solely* on the willingness of the Soviets *not* to attack us? And, if that hope fails, have nothing else to fall back on? That is the peace now being prepared for us by the knaves who have scrapped our strategic defenses.

Our Defenses Against Soviet Attack?

The gravediggers' strategy is proved by their near-hysterical refusal to permit the United States to have any defense against a massive Soviet nuclear attack. They have consistently refused to permit us to have an adequate civil defense system or an anti-missile defense system. Frequent Pentagon announcements of "development" of an anti-missile are merely "managed news" stories to hide the fact that McNamara has blocked *production* of any anti-missile or anti-satellite system.

The gravediggers have two principal arguments for not permitting us to have adequate defenses against a nuclear attack. First, they say that such a defense system is technologically and practically impossible. This is disproved by McNamara's own 1965 testimony when he conceded that a good civil defense system would save 29 million lives, and an anti-missile and bomber defense system would save 42 million more lives, or a total of 71 million American lives. Yet, McNamara is not spending the money to save these people. His position is, in effect: if we can save only 71 million lives, why bother to save any? No police force can give us 100% protection; but that is no reason for acting like McNamara and having no police.

If we were safeguarded by civil defense and an anti-missile system, we would not have to fall back on preemptive surrender or accept any surrender ultimatum. *More important,* if we were thus safeguarded, the Soviets would not launch their attack because they could not kill enough Americans in a surprise attack to make it worthwhile to go through with their strike from space.

The second argument the gravediggers use against a missile defense system is that it is provocative, it would make the Soviets think we are not peace-loving and would accelerate the arms race. Thus, Pugwasher Jerome B. Wiesner, top science adviser to the Kennedy-Johnson Administration, opined in *Scientific American:*

> "one of the potential destabilizing elements in the present nuclear standoff is the possibility that one of the rival powers might develop a successful anti-missile defense."[11]

Common sense tells us that this is just gravedigger doubletalk. There is no way it could possibly be destabilizing, or upset world conditions, if the

United States developed an anti-missile defense. The only thing this would destabilize is a plan for preemptive surrender. Self-defense is never provocative! The United States has never been the aggressor in any of the 4 wars we have fought in the 20th century. We did not start a war — even when we had a nuclear monopoly.

Wiesner is just as positive against a civil defense program. His article proves he knows the Soviets have a strategy of surprise attack, because he says that, if we had an anti-missile system and good civil defense, the Soviets would be compelled to consider these acts as portending a first strike against them. The facts are that the Soviets have an anti-missile system and excellent civil defense, therefore, we should logically conclude that they are planning a first strike against us!

Having made the decision *not* to build an anti-missile or civil defense system, the gravediggers were faced with the problem of how to put this over on the American people. In order to help them decide how best to do this, the Pentagon Whiz Kids ordered a confidential survey made by the National Opinion Research Center of the University of Chicago. Although made in the fall of 1964, this survey was kept secret from the American people until discovered by an enterprising reporter for *Missiles and Rockets* and published August 16, 1965.

This survey revealed that 80% of Americans believe that we should have something that can shoot down missiles attacking our cities, in other words, an anti-missile system; and 87% consider it desirable to place anti-missiles around all larger U.S. cities.

The most significant single finding in the 126-page report is that 66% of the American people believe the United States *already has* an anti-missile system — which we most assuredly do not! Therefore, the gravediggers have it easy. McNamara can go right on claiming that the United States is 4 times stronger than the Soviets, and the American people can go right on believing we have an anti-missile system while the gravediggers know we have *no* anti-missile system.

That wasn't all this secret Pentagon survey discovered. Each person polled was asked 99 questions, many of which were designed to give the gravediggers vital information about public attitudes so they will know how to make an anti-missile system sound so unattractive that the American people, without realizing the stakes involved, may reject it. The survey suggested a whole bundle of phony "hazards" connected with an anti-missile system, designed to make it sound expensive, difficult and dangerous.

First, the survey scared people with the possibility of accidental firing of the anti-missile. The person polled was given a set of statements to indicate whether he strongly agrees, disagrees, or is in between, including:

1) "Such [defense] missiles will make the Russians think we're going to start a war; therefore they might start one.

2) "I would feel that it is unfair that some cities are defended when my city is not."

Secondly, the survey created more doubts by suggesting many bad side effects such as:

"if the real estate values went down a little; if the radar . . . may cause poor television reception around here; if it means that we must set up shelters for everyone; if there might be some local opposition; if they take up a lot of acres that could be used differently."

Now the gravediggers know how to manipulate public opinion so that, if news of their failure to build an anti-missile system leaks out, they just cry "Wolf, wolf" with a fistful of "hazards" from this survey, and they can proceed with their secret strategy. Such news management poses no problem for an Administration which has already admitted that "it's an inherent government right, if necessary, to lie to save itself."[12]

There is just one thing the super-intellectual gravediggers haven't discovered. The knaves who are willing to accept "peace" by preemptive surrender may themselves be the victims of a typical Communist doublecross. There is no evidence to indicate that the Soviets would accept the surrender of America. To control a defeated United States would pose problems of police, transportation and administration which the Kremlin could not cope with and might not try. Even if a surrender were offered, the chances are that the Kremlin would still carry out its plan to *strike from space*. The men who would rather be Red than dead would end up being both Red *and* dead.

chapter XI

CREATING THE CLIMATE

Botanists know that each plant flourishes best in a particular climate. One of the tourist attractions in St. Louis is the Climatron — a huge domed greenhouse where scientists have created different "climates" for a living display of many beautiful plants which could not grow in midwestern weather.

In order to create the intellectual "climate" in which their plan to destroy U.S. nuclear strength can ripen before it is discovered, a number of *gravedigger fronts* promote various shades of "rather Red than dead" among the general public, in intellectual and academic circles, and in the halls of Congress. These fronts are largely controlled by the gravediggers, but most of those who do the leg work have no more grasp of the gravediggers' plot than the gardeners who tend the flowers in the Climatron understand the blueprints of the engineers who designed this modern marvel.

The Insane Policy Committee

The National Committee for a Sane Nuclear Policy, known as SANE, is the chief vehicle for mass propaganda against American nuclear weapons. It was born of a fusion of the ban-the-bomb views of Adlai Stevenson and Dr. Linus Pauling. The word "SANE" is a two-edged sword: it says that all those who are for banning the bomb are sane; it implies that all those who favor U.S. nuclear superiority must be insane. "SANE" was the brainchild of Dr. Erich Fromm, also noted for writing an afterword to the anti-Communist book *1984*, in which he tries to tell the reader that George Orwell wasn't really talking about Communism when he described the evils of state thought control in his classic book.

Other liberals who joined SANE at the outset were the UN's Trygve Lie, Lord Bertrand Rather-Red-than-dead Russell, and Mrs. Eleanor Roosevelt. SANE uses Dr. Benjamin Spock to appeal to women, Steve Allen for TV-viewers, Professor H. Stuart Hughes to appeal to the academic world, and Norman Cousins for the leftwing literati. Hughes explicitly urges us to destroy our nuclear weapons whether the Russians do or not in order to show we have faith the Soviets will not attack us.[1]

SANE spreads its anti-nuclear message through full-page newspaper ads, "peace" posters in subways and on train platforms, public rallies, local committees, peace demonstrations, Easter peace walks, and a semi-monthly newsletter. SANE plays on human emotions as an artist plays on the violin. It takes second place to none in the raw emotion in its ads, such as the profile of the pregnant woman and the caption "$1\frac{1}{4}$ million unborn children will be born dead or have some gross defect because of Nuclear Bomb Testing";

"Your children's teeth contain Strontium-90"; the bottle of milk with a skull and crossbones on it; a picture of John F. Kennedy with the caption "The next time madness strikes, couldn't it be The Bomb instead of the bullet?"; and, of course, the champion tear-jerker "Dr. Spock is Worried."

SANE even has its finger in the movies. A picture in *Sane World* of January 1965 shows Max Youngstein, producer of *Fail-Safe*, receiving the SANE Peace Award because that movie is "reaching millions of people both in this country and abroad with SANE's message on the dangers of the arms race." The main speaker of the evening was Adrian Fisher, Deputy Director of the U.S. Arms Control and Disarmament Agency.

Does it really matter what these ban-the-bomb propagandists are saying in their ads and posters? Can't we forget about them as "Rather Red than Dead" extremists, far out of the mainstream of American public opinion? For the answer, look at the boasting in SANE's own publications:

> "Most of the steps once advocated by SANE have now been adopted as policy by the U.S. Government. . . ."[2]
> "In 1957, SANE was organized and called for the end of nuclear weapons tests. In 1958, a treaty ending tests became United States policy, and in 1963, a treaty ending tests in the atmosphere, in space and under water was signed.
> "In 1958, SANE called for general and complete disarmament. In 1961, the U.S. Arms Control and Disarmament Agency was established. World disarmament became the policy of the U.S. Government.

"In 1960, SANE called for planning to convert our economy to a peace-time emphasis. In late 1963, President Johnson created a Committee on the Economic Impact of Defense and Disarmament and proposed to cut the defense budget by $1 billion.

"In 1961, SANE emphasized the futility of civil defense. In 1963, civil defense was eliminated or drastically reduced in the state of Oregon and in several major cities."[3]

By waging special campaigns against civil defense and anti-missile-missiles, SANE has joined in the gravediggers' campaign to keep America defenseless against a strike from space.

The Off-Center Study

An indispensable factor in creating the climate is to have a "foundation" — a rich, free-flowing gusher of tax-free money to finance books and publications, sponsor prestige meetings, and discreetly subsidize those in education, communications, religion, and even Government, who will spread the gravediggers' message. The perfect answer turned out to be the Center for the Study of Democratic Institutions. It soon began to play the same role in promoting U.S. unilateral disarmament that the notorious Institute of Pacific Relations played in the 1940s in persuading the U.S. State Department to assist the Communists to take over China.

The Center, a wealthy offshoot of the Ford Foundation with lineage through the malodorous Fund for the Republic, defines itself as an "intellectual community." The Honorary Chairman is

Paul G. Hoffman, who has made a life career of losing other people's money: at Studebaker, as U.S. foreign aid czar, and now with the UN Special Fund. The Chairman of the Board is William O. Douglas, Supreme Court Justice who advocates recognition of Red China but non-recognition of God in our public life and public schools.[4] The President is Robert M. Hutchins who, when asked by an official State legislative investigating committee how much he knew about Communism, replied under oath: "I am not instructed on the subject."[5] In 1964 Hutchins wrote: "My candidate for President is Norman Thomas. I voted for him in 1932 and I'd like to do it again."[6]

The Center's own list of Directors, Consultants, Staff Members, Participants in Publications, or Recipients of Grants, shows how far-reaching are the tentacles of this foundation in education and communications. This list includes Professor Linus Pauling; Henry Luce of *Time, Life* and *Fortune;* Reinhold Neibuhr of Union Theological Seminary; George Gallup of the Gallup Poll and Elmo Roper of the Roper Poll; Harvey Wheeler and the late Eugene Burdick, co-authors of *Fail-Safe;* Eleanor Garst, co-founder of Women Strike for Peace; Barry Bingham, editor of the *Louisville Courier-Journal;* Cyrus Eaton, moneybags of the Pugwash Conferences; Erich Fromm, friend of SANE; Justice William J. Brennan, Jr. of the Supreme Court; Arthur Larson, chairman of the discredited National Council of Civic Responsibility, a hypocritical front which claimed to be impartial and available for tax-deductible gifts, although it was secretly subsidized by the Democratic National Committee; nuclear strategist Henry A. Kissinger; Hans Bethe, Pugwasher and participant in another gravedigger conference called "Scientists on Survival"; Stanley Kramer, director of the movie *On the Beach;* Mike Wallace and the late Edward R. Murrow of television; James Reston of the *New York Times;* Adam Yarmolinsky, the man who had the strangest background and the most sensitive job in the Pentagon; Walter Reuther; and Hubert Humphrey.[7] The President's Report in 1962 listed Robert S. McNamara as one of the 54 Founding Members who "contribute $1,000 or more each year."

The senior gravedigger on the staff of the Center for the Study of Democratic Institutions is Walter Millis, author of numerous books and pamphlets urging the dismantling of American military strength. In his pamphlet *Permanent Peace* published by the Center, Millis says:

> "*If the price of avoiding all-out thermonuclear war should prove to be acquiescence in the 'Communist domination of the world,'* or any other of the unpleasant imaginings against which we cling, futilely, to the war system to preserve us, *it seems probable that the price will be paid.*"[8] (emphasis added)

The Vice President of the Center is the same W. H. "Ping" Ferry who, at the Democratic Party's Western States Conference in Seattle on August 6, 1962 made an attack on FBI Director J. Edgar Hoover so outrageous that Attorney General

Robert Kennedy immediately apologized to Mr. Hoover for the insult. On January 13, 1960, the Santa Barbara *News-Press* printed a long letter to the editor by Ferry urging the U.S. to junk all its weapons "of whatever kind," and "accept as a possibility" that "this country would be taken over by the Reds" as well as Western European countries. Though such a future is a "desperate and repellent vision," Ferry nevertheless finds it "thinkable" and urges unilateral disarmament upon us as "an alternative to our present policy."

Is the Center influential? Justice William O. Douglas boasted that more than 2,000,000 copies of its pamphlets and reports are now in circulation; and that "the faculty and students of hundreds of educational institutions — ranging from large universities to high schools — are using the publications as reference material and classroom texts."[9]

Council for a Slave World

The gravediggers look upon Congress as an anachronism from the horse-and-buggy days. They think it frightfully inconvenient that this constitutional stumbling block stands in the way of unilateral disarmament. Senators William Fulbright and Joseph Clark candidly expressed their views in a pamphlet entitled *The Elite and the Electorate* published by the Center for the Study of Democratic Institutions. Fulbright urged that Congress be stripped of its authority to check the President. Clark was unrestrained in his attack on all American legislatures, city, state and national, and indicated they are deserving of "scarcely concealed contempt."

In 1962 the gravedigger scientists produced a lever specially designed to bring Congress in line with their schemes. Called the Council for a Livable World, this lobby was founded by the late Dr. Leo Szilard, a gravedigger physicist who had previously made news at the Pugwash Conference of 1961 by proposing a personal nuclear peace treaty under which any American who violated its terms would be declared an "outlaw" to be shot on sight; and any American who informed on an "outlaw" would be given a $1 million tax-free award. After giving many lectures at colleges and universities, Szilard decided to concentrate on influencing Congressmen by cash.

The "1965 Action Program" published by the Council for a Livable World defines its No. 1 objective as: "Support election campaigns of thoughtful and responsible Congressional candidates." "Thoughtful and responsible," of course, means candidates who are working for U.S. disarmament and cuts in our defense budget. In 1962 the Council was responsible for contributing $45,-000 to the campaigns of 8 Senatorial and 10 Congressional candidates. The Council's favorites were Senators George McGovern, Joseph Clark, Frank Church, Wayne Morse and William Fulbright. Candidates they opposed were men such as Senator Peter Dominick. In 1963, the Council was responsible for special off-year contributions to a select list of approved Senators. In 1964 the Council supported, to the tune of $100,500, 18 candidates for the Senate and the House, of whom 14 were victorious.[10]

The second Council objective is to: "Provide advice, testimony, and study papers on important issues and support seminar programs for Congressmen and their aides." In practice, this includes ghostwriting speeches and articles on disarmament for Congressmen.

The Council for a Livable World also "maintains contact with members of Congress and the Administration who are deeply concerned with the need for arms control and disarmament." This means that the Council is, frankly, a lobbying organization for U.S. disarmament and, according to *Congressional Quarterly*, was the 4th highest spender of all lobbies during 1964.

By giving *first place* in its specific agenda to:
"Press the United States Government to maintain its position against deployment of an antimissile defense system,"

the Council has joined in the gravediggers' hysteria *against* defending America from a nuclear attack. If we had defenses against a nuclear attack, we would have alternatives other than a preemptive surrender.

chapter XII

LINING UP THE LIBERALS

The gravediggers are powerful, but not numerous enough to make preemptive surrender really "thinkable." So they have cleverly put to work others who are not privy to the plot. The whole liberal establishment was a natural for this purpose. A few gravediggers have activated the many liberals as a tablespoon of yeast raises a bowlful of batter.

The prime reason for the success of this tactic is that the liberals, individually and collectively, desire world government, or a reasonably exact facsimile thereof, such as an all-powerful UN, or NATO expanded into an Atlantic Community. This "one-world syndrome" is an attempt to escape from the problems of the present by working for a future utopia. One-worldism has been taught for so long in the schools, and idealized for so long in all liberal books and publications, that it is a tenet of their faith.

All the gravediggers had to do was tell the liberals that disarmament is the best way to achieve world government, and they were hooked! When leading gravedigger Walt Rostow wrote in his CIA-subsidized book, *The United States in the World Arena*, that he favors "an end to nationhood," this password put all the liberals in his camp. Publications of the United World Federalists clearly show that they look upon disarmament as the first step into world government. The common-law marriage between the gravediggers and the world-government liberals was formalized in November 1964 when SANE officially approved merger with United World Federalists.

The second reason why the gravediggers can exploit the liberals is that both are emotionally incapable of effectively opposing the Communists. Whittaker Chambers described their psychology this way:

> "Every move against the Communists was felt by the liberals as a move against themselves. If only for the sake of their public health record, the liberals, to protect their power, must seek as long as possible to conceal from themselves and everybody else the fact that the Government had been Communist-penetrated."[1]

In 1961 the *Fulbright Memorandum* revealed that Chambers' analysis is still true. The text expresses Fulbright's political fear that, if the American people are alerted to the danger of Communism, they will equate Communism with Socialism, and then they may equate Socialism with the "Administration's domestic legislative program."[2]

James Burnham, in his brilliant analysis of the liberal mind, explains further:

> "What Communism does is to carry the liberal principles to their logical and practical extreme; . . . The liberal's arm cannot strike with consistent

firmness against Communism, either domestically or internationally, because the liberal dimly feels that in doing so he would be somehow wounding himself."[3]

"Too Liberal to Fight"

The third reason why the gravediggers are able to line up the liberals is that they are, as Khrushchev told Robert Frost, "too liberal to fight."[4] Many of the most influential liberals declined to accept the invitations of their draft boards. After Vice President Hubert Humphrey was classified 1-A, he obtained a deferment because he was the campaign manager for the Democratic candidate for Governor of Minnesota. After his candidate lost, he requested another deferment as "labor consultant." As a trained pharmacist, he would have been more valuable in battlefield first-aid stations.

Supreme Court Justice Abe Fortas, who was 31 and without dependents on December 7, 1941, took advantage of his Federal position to secure a series of deferments for himself. Presidential Aide Theodore Sorensen escaped duty in the Korean War as a conscientious objector.[5] Robert Lowell, a favorite White House poet,[6] and Bayard Rustin, a leading liberal demonstrator,[7] both served prison terms for draft evasion.

When we were fighting on the same side as the Communists, deferments were not granted to men who "got religion" when they received their draft notice. But after the Communists started shooting us in Korea and Vietnam, the Supreme Court ruled in *U.S. v. Seeger* that a draftee can now escape military duty by, in effect, claiming he is too liberal to fight — even though his claim is not based on any religious conviction such as the Quakers have, and he is, like Seeger, "without belief in God, except in the remotest sense."[8]

The result is the disgusting demonstrations about Vietnam: the mobs halting troop trains, the burning of draft cards, and the anonymous phone calls to widows of our men killed in Vietnam saying "Your husband got what he deserved . . . I am glad . . . it serves him right." Even worse are the handbooks for draft evaders and "draft-dodger schools" instructing boys how to become a conscientious objector, how to self-ordain as a minister of an ad hoc church, how to flunk the physical by taking certain pills, and how to give answers which will disqualify as a homosexual or dope addict. To evade the draft, some boys have even advertised for unmarried, pregnant coeds "desiring partner in marriage."[9] These things are all parts of the agitprop campaign to sell our youth on the idea that we should not stop Communist aggression which, of course, plays directly into the gravediggers' plan.

Falling For the Fallacies

The fourth reason why the gravediggers find it easy to use the liberals is that the liberals are prisoners of their own cliches. Here are a few examples:

"Detente." This is a $5-word meaning the cold war is over and the Soviets have abandoned their aggressive intentions. As "proof" of "detente," the liberals cite Khrushchev's removal of his

offensive missiles from Cuba in 1962, and his signing the Moscow Test Ban Treaty in 1963.

In truth, the former was a deal and the latter was a defeat. The Administration still denies it was a deal, but this was exposed as a big lie when former State Department Director of Intelligence and Research Roger Hilsman gave all the details of how the deal was made in a naive article in *Look Magazine*.[10] Administration leaders were so furious about his revelation that they petulantly cancelled any further access by him to classified material.

In return for taking 42 of his missiles off their launching pads (there was no proof of their removal from Cuba), Khrushchev won: (1) the actual removal of 105 of our missiles from Turkey, Italy and England, (2) the promise that the U.S. would protect Castro from invasion by *anybody*, even by Cubans, and (3) the scrapping of our Monroe Doctrine in accordance with Khrushchev's demand, "now the remains of this [Monroe] Doctrine should best be buried, as every dead body is, so that it does not poison the air by its decay."[11]

The Moscow Test Ban Treaty did not show a sincere Soviet desire for detente but, instead, condemned us permanently to second-place in the strategic super-weapons race. The Joint Chiefs of Staff testified:

> "If . . . both sides faithfully observe its [the Moscow Test Ban Treaty's] provisions . . . the United States would not be able to overtake the present advantage which the U.S.S.R. prob-

ably has in the high-yield weapons field, whereas the Soviets, by underground testing, could probably retrieve in time any lead which we may presently have in the low-yield tactical field."[12]

"Nuclear stalemate." This is a sophisticated slogan based on the theory that science has come to a halt, nuclear weapons can't get any more terrifying or effective than they are now, so we can rely on an "existing nuclear balance of terror" to keep the peace. Liberal Congressman Melvin Price, Chairman of the Research and Development Subcommittee of the Joint Congressional Atomic Energy Committee, put it this way: "We are entering a leveling-off period, a plateau in the total dimensions" of the Government's research program.[13]

This is merely a new version of the liberal line of the 1930s that the United States was a "mature" economy, facing a future of perpetual high unemployment because we had reached a plateau of no further growth in industry or population.

The economic theory was wrong then, and this same military theory is wrong today. There is no ceiling on the ingenuity of man and the scientific improvements in store for us in the future. In science, industry, medicine, transportation, and war, those who rely on stalemate are doomed to failure. A few years ago, some airlines thought the DC-3, the most widely-used aircraft, was a plateau of achievement which could not be surpassed. Today the jets have made it obsolete. In 1939 the French were supremely confident that they had a weapons stalemate with the Germans.

In 1940, superior German planes and tanks crushed in 6 weeks what was thought to be the best army in the world.

"Nuclear stalemate" exists only in the imagination of the liberals. The U.S.S.R. is not satisfied to equal the megatonnage of U.S. weapons, but has developed weapons many times more powerful than our largest, the Titan II.

"*The real threat is Red China.*" Liberals love this illusion because it excuses their soft attitude toward Soviet Communism starting with recognition of the Bolsheviks in 1933. *Life* Magazine advised its readers that the biggest menace is — not the many super bombs the Soviets have today — but the one super bomb China *may* have in 1975, and that "Mao does not understand it."|[14]

The fact is that Red China's total stockpile of nuclear explosives is less than a single megaton, it has *no* arsenal of operational nuclear weapons, and *no* long-range delivery system. The Soviets have more than 100,000 megatons of nuclear weapons, and delivery systems consisting of ballistic missiles, orbital space vehicles, Bison and Bear bomber planes, and nuclear submarines. The nearest Chinese base is 7,000 miles; the nearest Soviet base, Cuba, is 90 miles. The Soviets have no doubt about the outcome of a conflict between a nation having a superabundance of nuclear weapons and one which has not. Such a country, the book *Soviet Military Strategy* declares, "may be forced by mass nuclear missile strikes to surrender even before its armed forces have suffered any decisive defeat."

"East-West trade will promote peace." Liberals cling to the myth that, if we could just all get to know each other better, have more trade and travel with Red countries, peace would be assured. On October 19, 1965 the State Department confirmed that a *secret* decision had been made three months earlier to sell nuclear-power reactors to Communist countries of Eastern Europe — a deal described as a "multimillion-dollar breakthrough in trade relations between East and West."[15]

Wars are *not* fought because countries do not know each other. The long, bitter World Wars I and II, the American Revolution, and our Civil War were all fought between states which had extensive trade and travel relations with each other. These close relations did *not* insure peace, and often enabled the aggressor to strengthen his war machine before attacking. Most modern wars have broken out between countries with close trade relations.

"Well-fed Communists are not dangerous." This favorite liberal fallacy has no basis in history. A well-fed Communist, like a well-fed army, is much more dangerous than a starving Communist. Napoleon recognized this when he said "an army marches on its stomach." Russian and Chinese Communists keep their slave laborers on a starvation diet because this lessens the likelihood of revolt. In 1933 when Hitler and his Nazis were hungry, they were not dangerous because they did not have any weapons. By 1939 Hitler and his Nazis were well-fed and very dangerous because they were heavily armed.

The liberals argue that the Russian people love their new "affluence" and won't let their bosses start a war. But nuclear weapons are made to order for world conquest. The 200 million Soviet citizens have absolutely no way of restraining the masters of the Kremlin from pressing the "button." No doubt the Kremlin would announce that the U.S. had struck first, or was about to.

All these fallacies, voiced and repeated by the entire liberal establishment, provide an intellectual fabric into which the gravediggers weave their fateful plan — just as, in *A Tale of Two Cities*, Madame Defarge skillfully knitted into her daily handiwork the names of those marked for the guillotine. "Detente" is the perfect rationale for the dismantling of U.S. military strength; if you tell the American people "the war is over," they will want to disarm fast, as they did after World Wars I and II. "Nuclear stalemate" is a wonderful excuse for McNamara's failure to research and develop the strategic weapons of the future. Talk about Red China is a beautiful diversion to cover up the evidence of a Soviet surprise strike and to pretend the Soviets are our "ally" against China.

"East-West trade" fits like a glove into the gravediggers' plan to foster personal friendship with the Soviet bosses by choice gifts such as U.S. chemical plants. After the surrender, the Kremlin masters may remember kindly those who gave them so many valuable resources in the form of industrial plants and "expanded trade." In the popular liberal jargon — some people may indeed be "building bridges" to the U.S.S.R.

chapter XIII

NEVER ON SUNDAY

What is potentially the greatest enemy of both the Communists and the gravediggers? Our churches. A truly religious person of any faith is a natural enemy of Communism because the foundation of Communism is atheism. Religion is the philosophy of hope; to a religious person, his faith is worth every sacrifice. The gravediggers are all defeatists, and they do not believe anything is worth dying for. As George Kennan explained:

"Such warfare (and this was true even in 1917) involves evils which far outweigh any forward political purpose [such as preserving the freedom and independence of the American people] it might serve — any purpose at all, in fact, short of sheer self-preservation, and perhaps not even short of that."[1]

Instead of openly opposing the churches, the gravediggers and the Communists have separately engaged in bold plans to try to harness the momentum of religion and make it work *for* them — instead of against them. As a practical matter, this means trying to persuade the churches to support "peace through unilateral disarmament." The gravediggers and the Communists have failed to put their message in the pulpits on Sundays, but let us see how they have used the churches the other 6 days of the week.

Gravedigger influence in the Protestant churches first emerged in the open at the Fifth World Order Study Conference of the National Council of Churches of Christ assembled in Cleveland, November 18-21, 1958. This Conference received national publicity because it passed a resolution urging the recognition of Red China and its admission to the UN. Subsequently, to test Protestant opinion, the Committee of One Million Against the Admission of Communist China to the UN polled 50,000 American Protestant ministers and discovered that 87% were against Red China on both counts.[2]

Although it did not make the front pages, the much more far-reaching action of this Cleveland Conference was a Report called "The Power Struggle and Security in a Nuclear-Space Age." And guess who turned up as the Chairman of the Section which produced this Report — none other than Paul H. Nitze, our present Secretary of the Navy. This Report laid down the gravedigger line of unilateral disarmament — wrapped in language to appeal to Christians:

"The United States should assume greater *initiative* toward bringing national armaments under international inspection and control in a process directed toward their consequent limitation, reduction and eventual abolition. . . . We believe the United States Government should continue its present suspension of tests, *unilaterally if necessary,* for a sufficient period of time to permit full exploration of the possibilities of arriving at a definitive international agreement. . . . Since we as Christians could not ourselves press the buttons for such destruction, we must declare our conviction that *we cannot support the concept of nuclear retaliation. . . .*" (emphasis added)

"Initiative" is gravedigger code language for unilateral; it means the U.S. should do it first, and we *hope* the Soviets will follow suit, a theme expanded in Nitze's 1960 Asilomar Proposal. Rejecting "nuclear retaliation" means letting the Soviets know in advance that, if they hit us, we will not hit back — a clear invitation to an aggressor to go ahead and press the button, and a shocking step toward national suicide in the nuclear age.

Here are other features of the gravedigger line in the Nitze Report: In case the Soviets do attack us, we must not have a "rapid" response, which is now smeared as a "spasm reaction." Instead we must take more "time for political consideration," or what is now called the "pause." The great danger of nuclear war is from "misunderstanding or error," or what is now called "accidental war," — not, of course, from the Soviets. We must not be "provocative" or look upon "the present struggle as a conflict between good and evil." We should "extend trade and travel" with Red China and the Soviet Union.

The Nitze Report pins our hope for peace on nuclear disarmament brought about by U.S. unilateral initiatives with the Soviets following our example. The fatal fallacy of this argument is proved by the fact that, since Nitze first publicly promoted this argument, the U.S. has made many unilateral-initiative moves, and there is not a single verified instance of the Soviets following suit. Instead they have doubled the range of their missiles and increased their power by the equivalent of scores of millions of tons of TNT explosive power. We have scrapped all our medium and intermediate-range strategic missiles, 3/4 of our multi-megaton ICBMs, and nearly 2,000 bombers. But they have scrapped nothing at all.

After the full impact of the Nitze Report became known, the National Council of Churches denied it was official policy. When Nitze was appointed Secretary of the Navy, he tried to claim he did not agree with it. But what else could he say if he expected Senate confirmation? The undeniable fact is that this Report was published with Nitze's name as Chairman and no indication that he dissented in any way. No denials or disclaimers can change the fact that the seed of unilateral disarmament and other gravedigger ideas was planted at a Protestant Conference of tremendous importance, in a Report which was widely circulated and referred to the local churches in "a nationwide educational effort."

The seed is flowering in such ways as the poll taken in 1965 by the Fellowship of Reconciliation which reported that clergymen favor "negotiations" in Vietnam by a margin of more than two to one.[4] The seed is flowering in such ways as the advocacy of "Christo-Communism" by one of the most eminent theologians in the country.[5] The seed is flowering in such ways as the statement called *A Christian Approach to Nuclear War* signed by theologians from 5 leading seminaries which said:

> "We plead with the leaders of our government not to persist in piling up nuclear arms even if other nations are not prepared to agree to the same course, but to formulate and call on our people to support a program of unilateral withdrawal from the nuclear arms race."[6]

Although no one has taken a poll, it is probable that the same 87% of Protestant ministers who opposed the Cleveland Conference's resolution in favor of Red China, would also reject the Nitze Report on unilateral disarmament. Undoubtedly the overwhelming majority of church-going Americans would agree with this patriotic statement by the Reverend Charles S. Poling:

> "So long as savage, atheistic Communism is on the march, we must be strong enough to convince any nation that to attack us is the sure road to national suicide. Whatever the cost and sacrifice, we must maintain a military posture, sufficiently advanced and strong to defend ourselves and preserve this nation as a strong citadel of peace and freedom. . . . Let us not be deceived by the prophets of disarmament and 'peaceful coexistence.' "[7]

"Peace on Earth" — Communist Style

The gravediggers and the Communists began to close in on the Catholics in 1963 when Pope John XXIII issued his Encyclical called *Pacem in Terris*. It was greeted by immediate and loud acclaim in the Communist press all over the world. The Reds recognized the title "peace" as a handle they could seize to twist the Encyclical into the context of their worldwide "peace" offensive. Leading U.S. Communist Gus Hall issued this directive: "We must utilize this Encyclical to the utmost in the struggle for peace."[8]

Through their press and Party members, the Communists began to misuse and distort, in effect, to steal *Pacem in Terris* from Catholics and use it (1) to promote the unilateral dismantling of American military strength, and (2) to persuade the United States to pull out of Vietnam.[9] Every informed person knows that *Pacem in Terris* did not say, and Pope John did not intend, anything remotely like this. But that didn't stop the Reds from saying he did.

Was the Communist tactic successful? The Theoretical Journal of the Communist Party, *Political Affairs,* boasted:

"That so many peace actions and expressions through petitions, statements in full-page ads in newspapers, mass meetings, resolutions by unions, peace picket lines, "teach-ins," and other actions are taking place on almost a daily basis in some parts of the country is additional evidence of the mounting peace sentiment in our country. . . . It may be said that many, or possibly most of these events have some direct or indirect relationship to *Pacem in Terris.* Undoubtedly the Encyclical has been a major factor in achieving the signatures of some 3,000 religious leaders to a full-page ad in the *New York Times* and other newspapers, calling on President Johnson to stop the war in Vietnam."[10]

This impudent article in the top Communist magazine proves that Communist misuse of *Pacem in Terris* is a matter of important and immediate concern to Americans of *all* faiths, and to the very security of our nation.

The gravediggers developed their own strategy to misuse *Pacem in Terris*. They undertook to con Catholics into accepting the gravedigger line by hiding it inside ostentatious use of the Encyclical, just as the Cubans were deceived when Castro used rosaries, prayerbooks and requests for chaplains to aid in his conquest of Cuba. The Center for the Study of Democratic Institutions sponsored a prestige gathering February 18-20, 1965 at the Hilton Hotel in New York City called a "Convocation" on *Pacem in Terris*. Its message could be summed up as urging the unilateral dismantling of American military strength and the abandonment of Southeast Asia. For example, Dr. Linus Pauling called on the 2,000 conferees "to obey the exhortation of Pope John . . ." to get out of Vietnam.

The Center for the Study of Democratic Institutions is making a well-financed and widespread effort to promote the message — not of the Encyclical — but of appeasment and unilateral disarmament wrapped in the mantle of Pope John. The Convocation proceedings were video-taped and shown on 90 educational television channels.

After Pope Paul VI spoke to the United Nations, the Communists falsely claimed that his speech aided their campaign for "the peace movement in general, and the cause of forcing the U.S. government to quit Vietnam in particular."[11] Although an official spokesman for the National Catholic

Welfare Conference denied this and said, "I can t imagine any Pope naive enough to advocate unilateral disarmament,"[12] nevertheless Communist propaganda aimed at Catholics was already bearing poisonous fruit. David Miller publicly burned his draft card,[13] and Roger LaPorte publicly turned himself into a human torch to protest U.S. anti-Communist action in Vietnam.[14] Both were brainwashed victims of a leftwing Catholic newspaper. Father David T. Thomas, Assistant Chancellor of the St. Louis Archdiocese, publicly testified in defense of the pornographic and anti-anti-Communist book *Candy*, whose author also wrote the scenario for the anti-Air Force movie *Dr. Strangelove*.[15]

The outstanding theologian in the Catholic Church, Charles Cardinal Journet of Switzerland, eloquently described the immorality of unilateral disarmament because this would permit "the Soviets, by the threat of war, to hold the world in their hands." He gave this ominous warning:

"If the non-Communist bloc unilaterally disarmed, it would give the world to the Soviet Empire and would betray all the holy values, temporal and spiritual, which we ought to defend: this would be the evil of betrayal."

Cardinal Journet defended the moral position of peace through strength — the right of the West to "produce atomic weapons *in the hope never to have to use them*, but just to build a deterrent against the threat of the enemy." He pointed out clearly that "we cannot hope *not* to use them unless we are *actually ready to use them*."[16]

chapter XIV

PARTNERSHIP WITH THE POLITICIANS

To succeed with their plans, the gravediggers must have the politicians as partners. How to persuade the politicians to carry out the grave-diggers' plot was quite a challenge because politicians are usually advocates of a strong national defense.

During the Kennedy Administration, Vice President Lyndon Johnson had been almost the forgotten man around our nation's capital, and he had never been really accepted by the liberals. In November 1963 when he succeeded a popular young President with an abundance of "image," Johnson had less than a year before the next election in which to make an impact on the voters.

Johnson made up his mind that the only way to bring the liberals to his side, to sell himself to the voters, and to assure his own reelection, was to go all-out for a *Great Society.* This would provide much bigger "spend and spend, elect and elect" schemes, disguised as social welfare, than anything conceived by the New Deal, the Fair Deal or the New Frontier. By the time he put Hubert Humphrey on the ticket with him as Vice President, LBJ had come full circle to this point of view.

Johnson had just one problem — the Great Society would be fantastically expensive. So much money could not possibly come from tax increases — or even the most trusting voters would see through the fraud. Squeezing several billion dollars of fat out of the existing budget is not easy even for those dedicated to economy, which the liberals certainly are not. LBJ had no scruples against deficit financing, but feared the political repercussions of letting the budget top the magic figure of $100 billion.

At this crucial point, the gravediggers stepped into the picture. They alone had the answer to Johnson's dilemma. They dangled their bait in front of the new President and said: To build your Great Society, to finance the welfare programs that will guarantee your reelection and assure your place in history as the greatest humanitarian of all time, we will give you $2 billion in the fiscal year 1964-65;[1] we will give you $8 billion in the fiscal year 1965-66;[2] and after that we can promise you up to $12.8 billion per year.[3] Rushing in from left field were the gravedigger professors, such as Seymour Melman of Columbia University, who talked imaginatively of figures up to $22.6 billion.[4]

Where was the money to come from? From the strategic defense budget! The financial magnitude of this plan was first revealed in *Foreign Affairs* of April 1964 by Roswell Gilpatric, who had recently resigned as No. 2 man in the Pentagon and whose views "usually have coincided with those of Defense Secretary Robert S. McNamara."[5]

Newsweek later described it this way:

> "President Johnson had inherited from his pred-
> ecessors a budgetary resource of great potency —
> the great defense effort that the country has
> made since the Korean War. . . . That is the
> melon that Presidents Eisenhower and Kennedy
> have bequeathed to Mr. Johnson and which he is
> now slicing up skillfully."[6]

The gravediggers not only gave Johnson the defense melon which he could then slice up for
domestic political purposes, but they also gave
him the salt for his melon so it would taste good.
They provided him with the fables and the intellectual gobbledegook necessary to put over this
plan on Congress and the American people.

They even provided Johnson with enough
doubletalk to soothe his conscience and make him
think he is doing the best thing for our country,
as determined by their superior knowledge of
classified information. Obviously, this made Mc-
Namara the most popular official in Johnson's
Cabinet; who else could give his boss $2 to $12
billion per year to spend on his pet projects?

Meanwhile, the Communist propaganda ap-
paratus was already in high gear carrying out the
1960 *Moscow Manifesto*, which said:

> "In each country it is necessary to promote a
> broad mass movement for the use of funds and
> resources to be released through disarmament
> for the needs of civilian production, housing,
> health, public education, social security, scien-
> tific research, etc. Disarmament has now become
> a fighting slogan of the masses, a pressing his-

torical necessity."[7]

The success of this directive is shown by FBI Director J. Edgar Hoover's official 1964 testimony that:

"Currently, the Communist Party, U.S.A., is stressing such domestic issues as . . . the reduction of military spending with the diversion of such appropriations to a broad program of social welfare projects."[8]

Taking Money From Tanks and Bombs

Was the gravediggers' plan successful? Just look at the Federal budgets requested every year by the President and adopted by the Congress. All expenditures for strategic offensive and defensive forces — the only weapons which can prevent a Soviet surprise strike from space — are down 45%[9].

Can we really believe that a President of the United States would divert national defense funds away from strategic military strength, and into political projects? Listen to the words of Lyndon Johnson himself in his speech in the East Room of the White House to the National Conference on Educational Legislation:

"We spend over $50 billion a year on military preparedness. But armed power is worthless if we lack brain power to build a world of peace.... We are going to improve education. We are going to improve medical care.... We are going to improve economic opportunities. . . . We are taking money from tanks and bombs and we are putting it into minds and stomachs and hearts."[10]

In President Johnson's own words, there it is — proof that he is "taking money from tanks and bombs" and putting it into Great Society programs. This gravedigger-devised policy has already stripped our military forces close to the point of potential disaster. This is demonstrated in official reports concerning even the "conventional" forces on which McNamara and his Whiz Kids tell us they are concentrating; this is why our GIs suffered so many shortages in Vietnam in the spring and summer of 1965. The public, of course, is prevented from knowing this because most of the vital information is classified "secret."

Far more critical, however, are the gravedigger cuts in the *strategic* power of the United States. Because all attention is focused on Vietnam, no Congressional committee is investigating what the gravediggers are doing to the *only* type of defense which can protect us from a Soviet strike from space.

As the months go on, the gravediggers are able to pull their yoke tighter and tighter around Lyndon Johnson. They exploit "managed news," political tricks, and the fact that attention is diverted to Vietnam. Each month it becomes easier for the gravediggers to cancel another strategic military project, retire more bombers, deactivate more missiles, cut back more advanced research, and block U.S. development of space weapons.

At the same time, with each passing month, Johnson can taste the delicious political benefits of his slicing of the melon. Surveys and press reports indicate that Johnson's popularity is growing, rather than diminishing, since his whopping victory in November 1964. He has persuaded Congress to pass more controversial legislation in one session than any President in history — more drastic legislation than Roosevelt in the heyday of the New Deal.

Computer Politics

The explanation for his success is that Johnson has skillfully sliced the melon according to the art called "computer politics" — in which the political advantages of Federal spending for one group of voters are carefully calculated against possible injury to other groups.[11] The Great Society is a giant grab bag which has something for everybody — and each one thinks he is getting more than he is paying for. "Renticare" even insures the politicians against loss of votes from groups which might get restive and say "but what have you done for me lately?" It is a 40-year gravy-train for both those who are getting relatively luxurious housing at the expense of hardworking taxpayers, and the favored groups supplying the "luxury" housing under 40-year contracts with the Government.

Where is the opposition to this gigantic program of buying the people's votes with their own money? Under Roosevelt, Truman and Kennedy, there was always vigorous opposition from Republicans and from various groups of taxpayers. Yet, today, Johnson's opposition appears divided and weak.

Samuel Lubell, the only pollster who personally rings doorbells to find out what people think, explained this "mood of tamed acceptance among the nation's voters":

> "The key to the whole amazing Johnson performance has been a revolutionary new development — the emergence of the Federal Budget as the most powerful political weapon in the country. . . . First, into the $100 billion of Federal spending, Johnson seems to have included at least one subsidy or benefit — from Medicare to aid for education — which appeals directly to each major segment of the population. Second, the fact that these programs have been combined with a reduction in Federal taxes has generated the euphoric feeling among many voters that these benefits are costing the public nothing. As a result, the objections to Federal spending have been reduced to a new low."[12]

The rabbit in the hat is the way LBJ has accomplished the miracle of financing his multi-billion dollar Great Society *at the same time that he has reduced taxes.* With one hand he has doled out the giveaways; with the other he has undercut the old resistance to big Federal spending. This is how the gravediggers have whiplashed the Johnson-Humphrey Administration into a partnership to weaken the United States past the point of no return.

Will the huge sums now required to bolster the war in Vietnam upset the plan? Absolutely not. They will merely put a tighter squeeze on our *strategic* nuclear defense and advanced weapons. No amount of money spent on Vietnam will help our *strategic* nuclear defense a single dollar's worth. Bookkeeping for the Vietnam war will be kept separate by the Administration so that, if it becomes necessary to raise taxes, this unpleasant duty will be tied to Vietnam and not be allowed to become associated in the public mind with Great Society vote-buying projects. The Johnson Administration will still have available to it the $12 billion annually which it *should have been spending* on strategic military power.

When the Soviets launched Sputnik in 1957, the then Senator Lyndon Johnson said the situation was so critical that we should live each day as if it would be our last. "We have less time," he intoned, "than after Pearl Harbor."[13] Sputnik I carried a few light scientific instruments and a beep-beeping radio. Sputnik II weighed less than 50 pounds and carried a small dog into orbit.

Proton I roared into space on July 16, 1965, weighing 26,500 pounds and clearly demonstrating Soviet leadership in the space race. On November 7, 1965 the Soviets announced they have a rocket which can strike a target anywhere on earth from orbit in space. It is significant that they stressed the capability of this new orbital rocket to "deliver its blow *unexpectedly* to the aggressor."[14] This amounts to a claim of zero-warning capability, which indicates that the warheads of Soviet weapons for their strike from space may indeed be in the 1,000-megaton range.

But after Johnson and Humphrey have sliced the melon and tasted its political sweetness, we don't hear any more warnings from LBJ, and most of the other sources have been silenced by the power of the Administration or the power of money.

chapter XV

PEACE OF THE SLAVE

The liberals, the churches, and the politicians have their own separate plans for peace. The liberals try for world government. The churches strive for peace based on good will toward men. The politicians drive for any sort of peace, short of an obvious surrender, in which they can keep getting reelected. Many in each group aid and abet the gravediggers' plan to disarm America because each group has been deceived into believing that disarmament coincides with its own particular objective. Tragically, the only peace they can ever attain this way is the peace of the slave. The liberals, churches and politicians are all being double-crossed by the gravediggers who are using them as cogs in the wheel of their plan for disarmament which will leave us no alternative to surrender to Soviet Communism.

As the liberals rush headlong, like Gadarene swine, to destruction of the only type of Government which would permit them to continue to be liberals, they scoff at all warnings with a favorite refrain—if all these things are true, why doesn't somebody in the Government tell us? Surely most of our officials must be good Americans; why don't some speak out and reveal the plot?

The first answer is that there are really very few who know the ultimate purpose of the plot to disarm America. Good Americans inside our Government are deceived by the "curtain of credibility" because they *want* to believe in the loyalty of their co-workers. This is especially true in the Armed Services; it runs through all hands, from GIs to Generals. When their "superiors" adopt a program which is stupid or suicidal, they "invent" ingenious reasons to justify it. Many American servicemen in Vietnam have convinced themselves that we are putting on the whole show to provoke Red China into joining the war — so we will have an excuse to bomb her nuclear facilities before they can become a major threat to the free world!

The second reason is that there are plenty of patriots in our Government who tried to give us the shocking part of the picture they themselves could see from their official positions; but the liberals refused to listen to them and did their best to silence them. Arthur Bliss Lane was our distinguished U.S. Ambassador to Poland at the time Poland was betrayed to the Communists by our State Department. He cut short his brilliant career in our diplomatic service, wrote a book called *I Saw Poland Betrayed,* and traveled our country telling the American people what the State Department had done. Few bothered to listen; his book received the silent treatment, and he died broken-hearted.

General Patrick J. Hurley, our U.S. Ambassador in China, saw at first hand how the State Department was betraying our wartime Asian ally. He resigned with big newspaper publicity, hoping his revelations would awaken the American people. After a few weeks, it was all over; few cared.

In Cuba, U.S. Ambassador Earl E. T. Smith sent back accurate reports that Castro was a Communist, and warned our Government not to support Castro.[1] Nobody listened. Today Ambassador Smith is no longer with the Government; but William Wieland, the State Department bureaucrat who pigeon-holed Smith's reports, has been twice promoted.

U.S. Ambassador Whiting Willauer, the man who in 1954 engineered the successful overthrow of the Red regime in Guatemala, could have made the Bay of Pigs a victory instead of a defeat had he not been removed from the project by the State Department, and his advice disregarded. After revealing the inside story to a Senate Committee, he died broken-hearted.[2]

In 1963 when the Moscow Test Ban Treaty was the issue, the Joint Chiefs of Staff testified as clearly as they could — without losing their jobs — that it would freeze the United States in second-place in the field of strategic nuclear weapons. But few listened.

Today there are dozens of men who have resigned or retired from their positions in Government to warn us of the dangers we face, including Ambassadors, Cabinet officers, other high Government officials, Generals and Admirals. These men know what is happening; they have sacrificed their careers to warn us. Will the liberals, the churches and the politicians wake up in time? The evidence is much stronger and much clearer now.

chapter XVI

SCARE-WORDS

"The bogeyman will get you if you don't watch out." For centuries this scare-word has frightened small children into eating their vegetables, doing their lessons, and otherwise obeying their elders.

The gravediggers treat the American people like children not sufficiently "sophisticated" to know what is good for them. To make the American people fall in step with their secret plan, the gravediggers have built up an arsenal of scare-words to frighten us away from any clue that might lead to discovery of their plot. The threat conjured up by these scare-words is just as phony as the bogeyman, but the fear they produce is real enough to halt the thinking process of most American citizens. Here are the principal scare-words exploded by the gravediggers and the fall-out of fallacies they have scattered. Only after we have swept away the scare-words can we discover the formula for the peace of the brave.

Escalation

The number-one scare-word is *escalation*. We are told that the United States should not take a military stand against Communist aggression anywhere in the world because the resulting conflict might escalate into nuclear war. The gravediggers want us to believe that, even if we resort to rifles in defense of freedom, this automatically puts us on the escalator going up, up, past the point of no return into nuclear holocaust.

"Escalation" is the solution to one of the mysteries involving President Kennedy. On March 23, 1961, he went on television with a great and spirited speech to our nation promising that we would never surrender to Communist aggression in Laos, nor desert our allies there; and he said that, unless the Reds stopped their aggression, U.S. strength would be brought into action. He did not say exactly what action — but he had moved the Seventh Fleet to the area, and had mobilized Army, Air Force and Marine units throughout the entire Pacific area.

But the Communists stepped up their attacks — and the young President backed down. Averell Harriman was sent to negotiate a face-saving surrender in the form of a troika coalition. The Communists have since taken over 3/4 of Laos, having committed 2,700 violations of the agreement.[1]

Why did President Kennedy renege on his resolute promises? Had he risked the prestige and honor of the United States on a shallow bluff? Here is the authentic story told by one who was "in on the action."

When the Communists increased their aggression and violence in Laos, Kennedy held conference after conference with his advisers. He proposed to stop the Reds in Laos with U.S. airpower, sea-based power, Army and Marine divisions. Each time he made a proposal, his advisers made the same response: "But that would bring on escalation!"

Each expedient he considered, each turn he sought to take, was dead-ended by the same chorus of doom: "Escalation . . . escalation . . . escalation." Finally, in desperation and frustration, Kennedy shouted at his advisers:

Are you telling me that, despite the fact that the United States is the most powerful nation the world has ever known, there is nothing I can do — in this little war, in this little country, against small Communist forces — absolutely nothing I can do which will not risk incineration of the entire world in a nuclear holocaust?

Jack Kennedy had proved his personal courage in World War II — but he could not overcome the gravediggers' morbid chant of "escalation." So, Laos went down the drain and America reneged on its solemn promises — not because of Communist guns or Asian troops, but because of the scare-word "escalation."

After we backed down in Laos, the Communists moved into Vietnam. The actions Lyndon Johnson has been forced to take there clearly expose the sham of the "escalation" argument. Every action which Kennedy proposed in Laos has, in fact, been used by Johnson in Vietnam. Yet there has been no escalation even to small, tactical nuclear weapons, much less to strategic nuclear weapons or all-out war. This clearly demonstrates that Kennedy could have used U.S. military power to win in Laos — and no nuclear holocaust would have followed. And Laos could have been won with 1/10 the military might used in Vietnam.

The whole threat of escalation to the holocaust level is a phantom of the gravediggers' imagination. McNamara, Gilpatric, Nitze, all the Whiz Kids and substantially all the military experts and nuclear strategists employed directly or indirectly by the Government, believe we are in a "nuclear stalemate" which neither side can break out of, or even *wants* to break out of. In any limited war, the nuclear weapons of both sides would be on super-alert. Would Johnson or Humphrey or Brezhnev or Kosygin decide to escalate up the ladder to 149 million deaths in order to win in Vietnam? Would the U.S. do it if the Soviets invaded Europe? Would the Soviets do it to help Red China? No one would do it. Lyndon Johnson knows this because he emphatically twice stated: *"General nuclear war is impossible"*[2] In other words, if the strategic nuclear stalemate exists, the balance of terror is our guarantee against escalation.

But what if the "nuclear stalemate" is broken? It can be broken by America's unilateral disarmament. It can be broken by major expansion of the Soviet anti-missile defense; or a breakthrough in anti-submarine warfare which would neutralize our Polaris missiles; or by development of gigaton warheads with space vehicles to deliver them.

Suppose, therefore, the nuclear stalemate is broken by the Soviets (which is very probable) and that we do not know about it (which is almost certain). Under these circumstances, *the threat of escalation is even less!* Escalation would be impossible because any Soviet plan to take advantage of their breakthrough would depend on two decisive advantages: (1) striking first (that is, with undamaged strategic forces) and (2) striking with the advantage of surprise (that is, having the opportunity to destroy U.S. nuclear forces before we can launch them).

Surprise has always given the aggressor a tremendous advantage. In the Pearl Harbor attack, the Japanese lost 64 dead; the Americans had 3,303 dead and 1,272 wounded. The nuclear-space age has multiplied the explosive power of strategic weapons by 100 million each. Therefore, the only rational use by an aggressor of strategic nuclear weapons is to use them with the advantage of surprise. Henry Kissinger, the nuclear strategist who is consultant to the U.S. National Security Council and the Joint Chiefs of Staff, puts it this way:

> "Short of an extraordinary technological breakthrough, victory in an all-out war can be achieved only through surprise attack."[3]

The Soviets know that the nuclear age has weighted the odds decisively in favor of the side that commits a surprise attack. A period of escalation, on the other hand, would permit us to marshal our weapons and stiffen our will to fight. Only in the escalation situation would the Soviets have no chance at all of achieving surprise, and they might even lose the opportunity to strike first.

The escalation argument is based on the false assumption that the Soviets need a *reason* to attack. The Soviets already have the best reasons in the world: (1) to prevent the U.S. from launching the surprise attack on them which the *Moscow Manifesto* predicts, and (2) to establish world "peace" — as they understand it.

The escalation argument is a revealing admission that the gravediggers have scrapped U.S. superiority — because there is absolutely no risk of escalation to general nuclear war so long as the United States has *escalation dominance*, that is, as long as we have strategic superiority over the Soviets and they believe we will use it if necessary. We did not have escalation of poison gas during World War II, because Hitler knew the West had deadly gases and superior means of delivery. We did not have escalation during the Korean War, because we had many atomic bombs and bombers to deliver them, and the enemy did not. We did not have escalation when President Eisenhower sent our Marines into Lebanon, because the Soviets knew we then had the bases in the Mediterranean from which we could destroy Soviet Russia.

If a taxi driver gets into a dispute with never-defeated-heavyweight-champion Rocky Marciano about the fare, the taxi driver will not escalate the dispute into a fist fight because Rocky has superior weapons. But the taxi driver may escalate the dispute if his passenger is not big Rocky Marciano, but little Casper Milktoast.

If America builds and maintains superior strategic military strength at the top rungs of the escalation ladder, we need never worry about escalation, nor about defeat, nor about surrender.

Overkill

Second in importance among the gravediggers' scare-words is *overkill*. They say we already have more than enough nuclear bombs to blow every Russian off the face of the earth, so how could we possibly use more?

We could not have won World War II without overkill. We manufactured enough ammunition to put 65 bullets into every man, woman and child in the Axis powers. Why? Because some ammunition is used in testing, some in training; large quantities must be held at many fronts because we don't know where the enemy will attack; after battle begins, some ammunition does not perform as it should, some is lost, improperly aimed, or destroyed by the enemy. Overkill is vitally necessary so that, when it is a matter of life or death, we can be sure that one bullet, or one missile, will hit the right target at the right time.

In World War II we manufactured 2 *thousand* depth charges for every submarine the enemy had or could build. Although theoretically one depth charge could destroy one enemy submarine, 1,500 depth charges were expended on the average for each submarine "killed." Many more depth charges were in stockpiles, distribution channels and anti-submarine depots. Without U.S. overkill, enemy submarines could have swept our ships from the seas. We needed this *overkill factor of 2,000* to save American lives and win the war.

Now that the Soviets have an effective civil defense and anti-missile system, overkill is more necessary than ever so we can be sure that enough missiles and bombers will reach their targets. Overkill means insurance against our weapons being "too little and too late." It means defenses strong enough to assure the survival of a free United States.

Because of America's great productive genius, overkill is one of our best weapons. We cannot have strategic military superiority without also having overkill. We should not permit the grave-diggers to scare us with a word; instead, we should *use* overkill to scare the enemy from any attempt to incinerate 149 million Americans.

Proliferation

People in high places sound off more and more frequently about the terrible danger of *proliferation*. The gravediggers have parlayed this big word into a bogeyman that gives people nightmares. Disarmament Chief William Foster said that proliferation is as great a present threat to the United States as the Soviet arsenal of weapons, and will be greater in the future.[4] The secret 1965 Gilpatric Report has been reported to recommend that "a treaty to bar nuclear proliferation should be granted priority over other foreign policy objectives."[5]

The time to stop proliferation was in the 1940s before our enemies got the atom bomb. The liberals in power in the 1940s and early 1950s were so contemptuous of security that they allowed the Communists to steal all our atomic and hydrogen bomb and electronic secrets. This spawned proliferation of a truly dangerous kind — the kind which has given the Communists the power to bury us if we drop our guard. Even Red China was helped to build an atomic bomb by two American-trained nuclear scientists who defected: Joan Hinton and Dr. Hsue-shen Tsien. Proliferation today is a scare-word designed to prevent our *allies* from having the nuclear weapons that the liberals already permitted our *enemies* to have!

Why are the gravediggers so desperately eager to prevent proliferation? Let's look at the facts. If we have proliferation, all or nearly all of the next 10 nuclear powers will be our friends — not our enemies — namely, Canada, Australia, Switzerland, Italy, Spain, Israel, Norway, Sweden, West Germany and Japan. Even the Institute for Strategic Studies concedes that "All but one of the countries (Czechoslovakia) which will soon have a nuclear-weapons potential, lie outside the Communist bloc."[6] Thus, if we have proliferation, the score would become 13 to 3 in our favor instead of the present 3 to 2. Proliferation would help the free world and deter the Reds.

The gravediggers know that the secret Soviet plan depends on conquering Western Europe intact. If most of the countries of Western Europe have nuclear weapons, the Soviets could not take Western Europe without destroying it, which would itself defeat their plan. The gravediggers' hysterical cries about proliferation are a sure clue that they want to keep our allies disarmed so they cannot oppose Soviet aggression with nuclear weapons. Thus, the scare-word proliferation is used to permit the Communists to conquer the world with the least possible nuclear opposition — the only thing which could stop them.

Accidental War

Like the magician who persuades his audience to watch one hand while the other completes the trick, the gravediggers have cleverly put across the notion that our greatest danger is from *accidental war*, rather than from deliberate war. We are told that the mere possession of nuclear weapons will bring about a nuclear holocaust because someone will push the wrong button by mistake. This was the theme of *Fail-Safe, Dr. Strangelove,* and *On the Beach.* The fact is that our nuclear devices are surrounded by so many safeguards that some experienced men wonder if they can ever be fired if we do need them!

The real purpose of the "accidental war" line is to make us think that the danger from nuclear war is primarily from some American, rather than from the Soviets! The real danger we face today is not from accidental war, but from a deliberate surprise Pearl Harbor-type attack on the United States by the Communists after they think we are sufficiently weakened militarily that they can get away with it without being fatally damaged by our retaliation.

Provocative Posture

Provocative posture is the scare talk dreamed up by the gravediggers and promoted by the Pug-washers with the specific purpose of eliminating our first-strike weapons. They tell us we must not have any weapons which would really damage the enemy because the Soviets would consider that "provocative." This scare psychology has caused McNamara to give up all our missile and bomber bases near the U.S.S.R., pull all our nuclear bombers out of Europe, and cancel 3/4 of our first-strike weapons, namely 149 giant Atlas and Titan missiles, 1,400 B-47 bombers, 600 nuclear armed aircraft carrier bombers, and 30 B-52 bombers, and shut down 60% of our nuclear production.

Without our huge armada of strategic bombers at the time of the Cuban missile crisis, we could never have made the Soviets believe we would take effective action if they did not withdraw the missiles.

Spasm Reaction

The liberals have always had their own vocabulary to promote their pet projects and to ridicule or smear any opposition. Thus, if you oppose the recognition of Red China, you are *rigid*. If you favor it, you are *flexible*.

The gravediggers also have a special vocabulary, of course more sophisticated. Thus, if the Communists attack us, insult us, or interfere with our vital interests, and we react as would any normal American, the gravediggers say we are having a *spasm reaction*. The clear inference is that we are just making an automatic, senseless response.

By using the scare-word "spasm reaction," the gravediggers successfully buried the policy of "war-winning response" which kept world peace during the Eisenhower Administration. The best deterrent to Soviet aggression is for the Kremlin to have the *sure* knowledge that, if they attack, we will hit them massively where it hurts, with no "pause" or negotiations. Only this will take the profit out of aggression, and make them realize that they can only lose, and have no chance of profiting, by launching an attack upon the United States.

Confrontation

The gravediggers have the horror of a U.S.-U.S.S.R. confrontation that the Devil has of holy water. They constantly tell us that we must do everything to avoid a nuclear power confrontation such as occurred when the Soviets installed offensive weapons in Cuba.

Actually, confrontations strengthen the West and the absence of confrontations weakens the West. Because there was no confrontation when the East Germans and Poles revolted in 1953 and when the Hungarians revolted in 1956, freedom lost and tyranny triumphed. Because we confronted the Communists in Iran in 1946, in Greece in 1947, in South Korea in 1950, in Lebanon with the Marines and in the Formosa Straits with the Seventh Fleet in 1958, substantial victories were won for freedom.

In building the peace of the brave, our first task is to expose and eliminate all the scare-words which have prevented our finding solutions to the problem.

chapter XVII

STRIKING THE PROFIT FROM THE STRIKE

For a dozen years prior to the capture of our defense policy-making by the gravediggers, the United States had a single national strategy. It never changed. It never needed changing. It worked successfully to deter a Soviet attack and to guarantee peace. It was stated publicly in September 1960 by the then-retiring Chairman of the Joint Chiefs of Staff, General Nathan F. Twining:

> "The American capability for decisive, war-winning response to any attack must be kept sure whatever the costs. It is the only reliable guarantee of peace. Forces that cannot win will not deter."

Since 1960 the gravediggers have deprived us of a "war-winning response" and created the risk that we could not or would not retaliate at all. A Soviet strike from space might therefore be so profitable it would gain them the world. To deter the Soviets effectively, our task is to strike the profit from the strike. We can do this by adopting a strategy which convinces the enemy that, even if he launches a massive attack at us from space, he could not possibly profit — and probably would come out with a fatal loss because of what we

185

would do to him.

This can be done by the President of the United States by the stroke of a pen. It will not be provocative, cost billions, or take years of time we do not have. Yet this change alone gives us a good chance of stalling a Soviet strike for years. The first way to strike the profit from the strike is to:

Command our 41 Polaris submarines that, in event of a nuclear attack on the United States, they must not return to port until they have fired all their missiles at their assigned Soviet targets. The captain, officers and crew should be sworn to this in well-publicized orders which could not be revoked even by the President. The Polaris crews would be alerted to a nuclear attack on the U.S. by cessation of their own radio traffic, and then they could double and triple check by surfacing at night to tune in on other frequencies — even on commercial radio stations.

This would defeat the Soviet hope that they could attack the U.S. and *not* suffer retaliation. First, Soviet strategy is designed to destroy all land-based U.S. retaliatory weapons, to kill all Government officials with authority to order retaliation, and to prevent the order, if given, from reaching any remnants of our land-based systems or the Polaris fleet. The irrevocable advance orders would defeat this by insuring that the Polaris missiles will be fired *without* any order being given or received. Secondly, the Soviet strategy is to annihilate nearly the whole population so that it would be irrational for any official to give the fire order even if there is a survivor to do so. The irrevocable advance orders would defeat this by having the decision made in advance when it would serve the highly rational purpose of deterrence. We would convince the Soviets they could not escape the "automatic" response to their strike.

This "committal" of our Polaris forces would also serve to protect us from a Soviet nuclear post-attack blackmail attempt. Suppose instead of a complete genocidal attack, they planned to kill only half our people in the first attack, and then demand: "Turn over all your weapons, including your Polaris fleet, or we will destroy the remainder." The Soviets would be deterred from attempting such an attack if they knew we had put it out of our control to surrender the Polaris fleet, or to prevent their retaliating against the Soviets.

One great advantage of this committal of the Polaris fleet is that *no one can contend that it threatens the Soviets if they do not in fact actually launch an attack against the United States.* It in no way increases the possibility of so-called "accidental war" — because the Polaris irrevocable orders will require absolute verification that the U.S. had actually been devastated before firing.

Here are other steps we can take immediately and with little expense. Restore the strategic nuclear bombers to our 17 great attack aircraft carriers (which McNamara stripped), and put them back on "strategic alert." Admiral Arleigh Burke testified that these carrier bombers could, under certain circumstances, deliver more blows than SAC bombers.

Keep 1/6 of our bombers on a continuous alert. Our "obsolete" bombers — once in the air and dispersed from their bases — are far less vulnerable than the Minuteman missiles in their concrete and steel silos. Load our B-52 bombers with two 60-megaton bombs which McNamara testified we are capable of making.

If properly targeted and irrevocably committed like the Polaris fleet, these U.S. forces could assure the Soviets of a loss fatal to their plans for world conquest. A U.S. retaliatory strike of this size would wipe out most of the 800 Soviet medium-range missiles which hold Europe hostage, and would take out most of the Soviet army and reserves. Without this missile force and trained military manpower, the Soviets could not take over Western Europe. This would strike the profit from the strike because the Soviets would know they could not accomplish the most vital part of their strategy: to take Europe intact.

The "committal" of our Polaris fleet and the crash program outlined above would guarantee the survival of the U.S. for a few years. It would buy us the precious time we need to build the more powerful weapons to preserve our future freedom. The next task would be to resurrect all the great advanced weapons which American genius has developed, but which have been killed or stalled by McNamara, such as the Skybolt and Pluto. Mass production of Titan II missiles and new super-missiles is a must. We should build more Polaris submarines and rush production of the more sophisticated and powerful Poisedon missiles. We should mount Polaris and Poisedon missiles also on surface ships. We should protect the 71 million American lives — now unnecessarily exposed — by a good anti-missile system and civil defense.

Most important, we must go into immediate production on the B-70, both as a bomber and as a super-sonic commercial airliner. The U.S. would thus beat the French-British SST to the commercial market by 5 years and thereby gain enough on the billions of dollars airlines throughout the world would spend buying this from us for a super-sonic passenger plane, to pay much of the expense of the bomber project. A fleet of B-70 bombers — teamed with missiles and low-altitude bombers to suppress Soviet air defenses — could deliver the nuclear power to blast the Soviets off the face of the earth if they dared to strike us from space.

These programs would carry us with safety into the 1980s when our space armadas would be ready to take over. England kept world peace for decades and insured freedom for all Englishmen for centuries by supremacy in seapower. America can do the same through space power — if we abandon the Gilpatric space policy and determine to win the military space race. The U.S. moon program need not be cancelled — just postponed until we can afford a $30 billion non-military luxury. Wouldn't you rather spend those billions on space defense systems, space interceptors and orbital bombers to assure the safety of your home and family — than on a "prestige" splurge to send a couple of astronauts for a 12-hour visit to the moon?

For the second generation of space weapons, we will have a tremendous advantage over the Soviets — if McNamara has not already thrown it away. Project Orion embodied the most advanced space nuclear propulsion system ever devised, with great military as well as scientific potential. Congressman Craig Hosmer asserts that it was eliminated in order to maintain the U.S. "posture of nuclear pacifism."[1] A top U.S. scientist, Dr. Freeman J. Dyson, declared that the success of this space project "has rarely been equalled."[2] We invested 7 years of development time and money in it.

The above programs will keep America safe from the terror of a strike from space. It will also protect us from the paralyzing fear of "escalation" up to a nuclear holocaust. Since our new strategy will be strong enough to deter the enemy from launching a strike from space even with the advantage of surprise, it will deter with equal certainty a far more risky strike in a crisis situation in which *all* our forces would be alert. But what can save us from the Communist encirclement plans — their long-range plans to nibble-and-bleed-us-to-death, to conquer the world in installments, as in Korea and Vietnam?

And No More Small Wars

Mao Tse-tung's plan for world conquest is to conduct a "protracted war against the United States" by using 25 million trained troops in Southeast Asia "to keep capitalistic countries increasing defense expenses until economic collapse overtakes them." The gist of the Red Chinese plan is to submerge the "few million U.S. aggressor troops" in a "vast ocean of several hundred million Chinese people in arms." The original Mao plan was issued in 1953 in a secret version.[3]   In September 1965 it was updated in substance and reissued over the signature of Lin Piao, Chairman of the Chinese Communist Party Central Committee.[4] This time the Chinese Reds dared to make it public because, after Korea and Vietnam, they are sure it will work. And it will — *if* we fight according to their rules.

Their great resource is massed millions of conscripts. If we had another Korea super-imposed on a Vietnam, our manpower sources would soon run dry. But why fight according to their rules? This means sending thousands of American boys to fight, be tortured and die in remote places such as the hills of Korea or the jungles of Vietnam, in "limited" wars with no real hope of victory. The most they fight for is "negotiations" or "stalemate." Even this "solution" does not save their lives, because 3/5 of all U.S. casualties in Korea were suffered *after* Truman fired MacArthur and we sat down to negotiate at Panmunjom.[5]

On June 30, 1965, Senate Majority Leader Mike Mansfield denounced Republican leaders for wanting victory in Vietnam at "bargain basement rates in American lives."[6] Why, in the name of God, shouldn't we want victory at bargain basement rates in American lives? The most precious thing we must save is the lives of our sons. Will the

American people allow the gravediggers to keep sending our boys into a bottomless pit in Asian wars — instead of using the better weapons technology has given us?

We have had 20 years of experience which prove that a proper strategy for the use of large nuclear weapons will preserve the peace against major aggression. This doctrine of "massive retaliation" worked so well that Winston Churchill said there would not be one free man left in Europe, were it not for American nuclear power. This strategy cannot, however, prevent smaller wars such as in Korea or Vietnam. The Reds simply will not believe that a Korea or a Vietnam is important enough to the United States for us to risk massive retaliation. The threat is so disproportionate to the aggression and to our interest that it is not credible. The punishment must fit the crime. To deter smaller wars, we need a strategy of deterrence by smaller weapons.

Is this a new and dangerous policy? On the contrary, it was used by both Presidents Kennedy and Johnson — and it worked. And if adopted as permanent U.S. strategy, it can effectively prevent American boys ever being bogged down in another faraway "limited" war. In 1961 President Kennedy was confronted by Soviet threats — not against all of free Europe — only against West Berlin. He made a formal declaration that we had "calmly resolved" to employ nuclear weapons if necessary to defend Berlin.[7] The Soviets believed his warning, and we didn't have to use the tactical nuclear weapons. Apparently,

Lyndon Johnson has done the same thing in Vietnam — otherwise Red China would have sent in its troops to outnumber us 2-to-1, just as in Korea.

Today we have literally thousands of tactical nuclear weapons in Europe. Since Kennedy's death, the gravediggers have by implication abandoned his wise policy and thereby weakened the nuclear deterrent which had protected Western Europe. They have now retreated to the position that the use of these tactical weapons must be delayed until our NATO allies are on the brink of being defeated by a massive Soviet invasion. This sudden, unilateral change in U.S. strategy has shaken European confidence. They know that such a senseless delay invites aggression, instead of deterring it. They know that this would be too late and could only result in devastation. Knowledge of what this new U.S. policy means has brought NATO to the brink of a breakup. The NATO alliance has served as the sword and shield of the free world for more than 15 years — but we can hardly blame our NATO allies for preferring to deter a war rather than become a battlefield.

We must, therefore, restore the greatest value of tactical nuclear weapons — that of a *deterrent*. If we eliminate the gravedigger doctrine of the "pause" and instead realistically warn that our weapons will be available immediately if the Soviets attack, we will never need to use them. NATO will gain new life, unity, and power — plus a "credible" deterrent to preserve peace and freedom.

The unlimited nuclear power discovered and developed by America gives our nation the greatest opportunity in history to bring about world peace. By advance committal of our invulnerable *strategic* nuclear weapons to an effective retaliation, we can prevent both a surprise strike from space, and escalation of crisis situations into "big" nuclear wars. By the advance committal of the world's greatest arsenal of *tactical* nuclear weapons, we can effectively prevent aggressors from even starting little conventional wars because they will know they cannot win. This will guarantee that American boys will never again be bogged down in a Korea or a Vietnam; it will force Red China to abandon its published plan to defeat the United States by "submerging" Americans in vast oceans of hundreds of millions of armed Chinese.

What About Vietnam?

Our new twin strategies for deterring all new wars — big and little — would make immediately available additional strength for America. We would be able to bring home from Europe 4 or 5 divisions without alienating our NATO allies. Our having restored the credibility of the NATO tactical nuclear *deterrent* is far more valuable to them than any number of U.S. divisions. One or two divisions could be released from Korea also by the new strategy.

With such resources available, all we would need to win a decisive military victory in Vietnam would be adoption of an *objective of victory*.

If the Johnson-Humphrey Administration really wants to win, it could do so in the shortest time, with the fewest casualties, by eliminating the "privileged sanctuaries" and using enough trained professionals.[8] As Ho Chi Minh said, you can't kill a snake by stepping on its tail. You would not send 5 policemen to quell a raging riot. They would all be killed or hurt. Even 500 police might suffer casualties. Sometimes the National Guard must be called — and then the riot is quelled with the fewest casualties on both sides.

The effect on Vietnamese morale alone would be sensational. Our side would regain resolution and hope. The South Vietnamese have proved their courage for 10 years. The guerrillas would become discouraged and frustrated. Hope of being on the winning side is what keeps them going. With that hope blasted, many conscripts would switch to our side and villagers would cooperate.

All the American soldiers needed to win could be supplied without adding the 350,000 to the present U.S. armed forces as requested by Mc-Namara. The draft need not be increased, nor would we need to call up Reserves or the National Guard. Some $10 to $12 billion a year could be saved from the added costs of maintaining, training, and equipping untrained manpower. A third of a million young Americans could be spared the dislocation from normal careers in schools, colleges, and employment. The money thus saved could be invested in our most vital security need — rebuilding the strategic might of the United States to protect us against the Soviet threat.

Mao Tse-tung in late 1965 reached a new cres-
cendo of hate and threats in the *words* he hurled
at America. The great Chinese people he pledged,
would join the peoples of Indo-China in driving
the U.S. imperialist war-expanding aggressors
"resolutely, thoroughly, completely and totally"
out of Indo-China and "out of all Southeast Asia."

Words of one of the Communist giants frequently serve as a diversion to conceal the *actions* of
the other. With so much talk from *Peking* — what
was the *Kremlin* up to?[9]

The United States was in 1965 making the
same mistake in North Vietnam that we had
made in Cuba in 1962. Unlimited shipping was
being permitted to unload at Haiphong, the one
large port of the Communist North. The Soviets
were furnishing increasing numbers of the most
advanced types of weapons: surface-to-air missiles and radar-controlled anti-aircraft batteries.
These were taking an increasing toll in lives of
American airmen and U.S. tactical aircraft. But
still the Administration made no protest and had
no words of rebuke for the Soviets.

Were the Soviets taking the same advantage
of the Administration's failure to establish a
blockade that they took in Cuba? Observers
spotted the same Soviet ships, with the same
oversize hatches built especially to load long, nu-
clear-warheaded missiles — just like those they
sneaked into Cuba.

The Red Chinese were talking about driving
the United States out of Southeast Asia: Were

the Soviets the ones who were really getting ready to do just that?

Experience in Cuba should have taught us never to tempt the Kremlin to prepare a surprise for us. How would the situation look to Brezhnev and Kosygin — two of the three Soviet-Presidium level co-conspirators in the Cuban missile plot?

The risk of major damage to the Soviet Union would be far less. In the Cuban situation, the U.S. had a vast array of conventional power mobilized and poised for invasion of Cuba from Florida. Our supply lines were 90 miles long — not 7,000. The Soviet Union was in no position to bring any conventional military power to bear in Cuba — to oppose the massive U.S. forces. The threat the Soviet missiles posed to the United States was the most devastating ever faced by any nation. Yet we did nothing to penalize the attempt — nothing to discourage a second attempt.

Also, at that time we had far greater deliverable strategic megatonnage than McNamara has now left us. But we made no demands; asked no assurances against repetition. The White House praised the "statesman-like" conduct of the Kremlin leaders. If there had been no penalty, no risk, to the Soviets in the Cuban plot — why should they think they have anything to lose by trying again in Vietnam?

What would they stand to gain? Quite a step toward world conquest. Suppose they announced that they had supplied medium-range nuclear missiles to the fraternal Socialist state of North Vietnam, and demanded the withdrawal of foreign aggressor troops from all of Vietnam — to permit the Vietnamese to determine their own form of government.

What would we do then? What could we do?

If we gave in, we would lose every ally we still have in the world. All nations would seek the best deal they could get from the Soviets. Remember that we have not yet even adopted the committal strategy for Polaris submarines. We have no crash program for a substantial airborne alert — nor for restoring nuclear-weapon bombers to Navy aircraft carriers and strategic alert.

If we permit the Soviets to ship their nuclear missiles into Vietnam, we may be brought close to abject surrender or the nuclear destruction of more than 150,000 American soldiers and millions of South Vietnamese civilians.

But now we can prevent the situation from arising. We can prevent Brezhnev and Kosygin from repeating in Vietnam what they did in Cuba.

We learned something from Cuba, too. The Soviets will not go to war if we impose a blockade. Time is running out. Time for the blockade . . . time to eliminate the privileged sanctuaries in North Vietnam and to stop, as General LeMay said, "pecking around the edges" and "hitting the wrong targets"[10] . . . time to rebuild American strategic power . . . time to avert surrender . . . time to save America.

chapter XVIII

PEACE OF THE BRAVE

At certain times in history, freedom and civilization have been saved because *just one individual* sighted the enemy in time. During World War II, one reconnaissance plane flew a few extra miles beyond its course and discovered on the horizon the Japanese fleet steaming toward Midway Island. Ensign Jack Reid's alert gave our Pacific forces many hours of advance warning not anticipated in Japanese war plans — time to bring U.S. planes from all over the Pacific. Historians now tell us that the great battle of Midway was the turning point of the war. The keen vision of one American pilot meant the difference between life or death for thousands. The brilliant work of another American naval officer, Captain Laurance Safford, in breaking the secret Japanese codes contributed not only to winning the Battle of Midway, but to many other U.S. victories.

America has been brought to the brink of peril by men who lack faith, who are defeatists, and who tremble at the mere mention of phony scarewords. The purpose of this book is to give the reader a lookout from which he can sight the enemy, alert his fellow citizens, and take the action necessary to mobilize our resources in time.

America has all the material and technological resources we need *to win any race* we decide to run against the Soviets. But that is not enough. Just as a lack of faith and courage brought America to a position of fearful peril, America can be saved only if we have enough citizens who are iron-willed, nobly dedicated and supremely unafraid. We must have the will to run the strategic arms race, the courage to stand up to the scare-words and the smear merchants, and the dedication to pursue our goal until we win the only kind of peace we can preserve with freedom — *the peace of the brave.*

Two events prove that there are enough Americans with the bravery to solve the problems of war and peace in the nuclear-space age. American leadership was tested during the whirlwind brainwashing campaign in 1963 to railroad the Moscow Test Ban Treaty through the Senate. The liberal communications media made a vote against the Moscow Treaty appear as a vote recklessly to risk nuclear war. Out of 100 U.S. Senators, 19 stood fast against that pressure campaign. Those were brave Senators indeed, and nobly dedicated.

A year later we had a massive demonstration that the American people have bravery in an even higher percentage. 27 million voters out of 70 million had the resolution, the fortitude and the old-fashioned bravery to vote for a candidate smeared by the greatest fear campaign in history. The most powerful political forces of all time tried to intimidate the voters with threats that Barry Goldwater would plunge the world into a nuclear holocaust. Lyndon Johnson implied in his campaign speeches that Goldwater's election might result in 100 million American deaths. Television showed little girls eating ice cream cones about to be incinerated if the viewers voted contrary to the Administration. Yet, 27 million looked this terror campaign in the face and worked with supreme dedication for the candidate they felt could save the nation.

The 27 million Americans — and the additional millions they must now enlist in their crusade — must again display their courage. They must be brave enough to face the campaign of nuclear terror and demand a new national strategy which will insure that nuclear power will be *the supreme power for good* — instead of the supreme power for evil. They must be brave enough to trust their own wisdom, and to reject the decisions of an Administration which explains wrong decisions by claiming superior knowledge based on "classified information."

Admiral Arleigh Burke, member of the Joint Chiefs of Staff longer than anyone else, gave his conclusion about *the importance of the American people* in making national strategy:

> "The existence of freedom will continue to depend upon the ability of free people to better understand their own national strategy in relation to the Communist challenge and to deal with this challenge in a positive, successful manner."[1]

Grassroots vs. Gravediggers

How can the American people deal with the nuclear challenge and prevent a strike from space?
1. *Faith.* We must nourish and sustain our

faith in God, faith in America, and in the ideals that made this a great nation. As Billy Graham said: "The world is on fire, and man without God will never be able to control the flames."[2] We must pray as though safety from Communist fire depends on God, and work as though it depends on us.

2. *Education.* Join in a great educational effort to enable your fellow citizens to "sight the enemy" while there is still time. God told Abraham that Sodom and Gomorrah would be spared if only 10 good men could be found. When 10 could not be found, fire and brimstone descended on those cities. America can be saved from a strike from space if we can find 10 good Americans in each community who will band together to do the necessary educational work.

3. *Political action.* Work your precincts with fidelity and devotion to assure the election of Congressional candidates and other Government and Party officials on every level who are *for* keeping America strong. "Fire the gravediggers" must become a slogan that every politician clearly understands.

4. *Public opinion.* The danger is so critical that we must work for a reversal of the gravediggers' policies *prior to* and *whether or not* the "ins" are turned out of office. This is *not* an impossible task. In 1962 public opinion forced President Kennedy to "do something" about Cuba. Millions of grassroots Americans deserve the credit for saving our country from a surprise attack by joining in the ground swell which literally forced the President

to reinstate the U-2 flights over Cuba. The American people must understand and learn the meaning of this 17-word formula for survival: *We can lose. We cannot afford to lose. We can win. We can afford to win.* Public opinion must demand that our leaders follow the time-tested advice of George Washington: "To secure peace, . . . it must be known that we are at all times ready for war."[3] General Thomas Power restated this in nuclear-age terms on November 14, 1965:

"The 3 basic principles of *deterrence* through military superiority are:

"1. Have the unquestioned capability to achieve a military victory under any set of conditions — in other words, *no bluffing.*

"2. Let all potential aggressors *know* about this capability and your determination to *use* it to maintain peace with honor.

"3. Today you no longer deter with the military force you have in being, but rather the military force that a potential aggressor *thinks* you will have left after he has subjected you to *the surprise attack* he is planning against you." (emphasis added)

5. *Missile Defenses and Bomb Shelters.* As long as LBJ continues to spend the money on the moon race that should be spent to save 71 million lives, then those who want to live in freedom must take action to secure the shelters and anti-missile defenses necessary to save so many Americans and thus strengthen our deterrent against a strike from space. The Nike X anti-missile system has already been developed and tested. It is terribly urgent that it be produced

and deployed as *unanimously* recommended by the U.S. Joint Chiefs of Staff.[4] All patriots must unite to reverse the veto of these marvelous defense systems by the gravediggers.

6. *Private development of defense weapons.* After British pacifists disarmed their country in reliance on Nazi promises, England was saved by grassroots citizens and by private, patriotic industry. Thousands of little boat owners crossed the Channel and evacuated the poorly-armed British Army from the beaches of Dunkirk. Against opposition from British appeasers, private industry had invested the lead-time and money needed to perfect two great inventions: radar and the 8-gun Spitfire fighter. The Battle of Britain was won by these two weapons developed by the initiative of private citizens Henry Tizard, Reginald Mitchell and their supporters. American industry should not wait for Government orders, but use the little lead-time left to improve our strategic offensive and defensive weapons.

In the nuclear-space age, Americans do not have the option of being slaves. Our choice is not Red *or* dead — but *freedom through strength,* or death by doing nothing. The "moment of truth" for each American is when he faces the evidence and dedicates himself to win the battle of the grassroots versus the gravediggers. America is not only too young to die — she is too strong to surrender.

REFERENCES

I. The World's Greatest Mystery

1. Testimony, Feb. 18, 1965, p. 47.
2. Robert Donovan, "Have We Learned the Lesson of the Bay of Pigs?" *Los Angeles Times* Service, printed in the *Honolulu Advertiser,* July 27, 1965.

II. What Happened to Khrushchev?

1. Nov. 6, 1964
2. Gettysburg, Oct. 20, 1964.
3. Oct. 26, 1964.
4. *Time,* Nov. 6, 1964, p. 26.
5. Ibid.
6. UPI Dispatch, Oct. 30, 1964.
7. *Washington Post,* May 15, 1963.
8. Richard Starnes column, Nov. 5, 1964.
9. Television speech, Oct. 18, 1964.
10. *Newsweek,* Nov. 9, 1964, p. 73.
11. Oct. 23, 1964, p. 29.
12. Ibid.
13. Harrison E. Salisbury, *New York Times,* Oct. 20, 1964.
14. UPI Dispatch, Moscow, Oct. 29, 1964.
15. Dispatch from Moscow, Nov. 6, 1964.
16. American Bar Association, *Peaceful Coexistence: A Communist Blueprint for Victory,* 1964.
17. *Washington Post,* July 6, 1960.
18. Department of State Bulletin, Feb. 6, 1961, p. 302; *Time,* Feb. 2, 1962.
19. Mar. 6, 1961.
20. Senate Internal Security Subcommittee, *Analysis of the Khrushchev Speech of Jan. 6, 1961,* Testimony of Dr. Stefan T. Possony, June 16, 1961, p. 50.
21. *Newsweek,* Sept. 23, 1963, p. 73.
22. Mar. 29, 1965, p. 54.
23. AP Dispatch, London, Aug. 15, 1964. June 21, 1963.
25. American Security Council *Washington Report,* 64-36, Nov. 2, 1964.
24. Speech at Plenary Meeting of the Central Committee,

26. Sept. 25, 1964, p. 19.
27. Alberto Ronchey, *Russia in the Thaw*, 1965, p. 161.
28. Chester Ward, "The New Myths and Old Realities of Nuclear War," *Orbis*, Summer 1964, p. 255.
29. Phyllis Schlafly and Chester Ward, *The Gravediggers*, Pere Marquette Press, 1964.
30. UPI Dispatch, Moscow, Mar. 15, 1965.
31. UPI Dispatch, Feb. 23, 1965.
32. *U.S. News & World Report*, Nov. 15, 1965, p. 82.

III. Make A Noise In Vietnam

1. *U.S. News & World Report*, Aug. 17, 1964.
2. UPI Dispatch, Washington, Feb. 12, 1965.
3. Escalation will be discussed in Chapter XVI.
4. *Elections in Petersburg*, Jan. 12, 1913, Sochineniya (Gospolitizdat, Moscow, 1946), Vol. II, p. 277.
5. American Security Council *Washington Report*, July 6, 1964.
6. AP Dispatch, Moscow.
7. *St. Louis Post-Dispatch*, Aug. 24, 1965.

IV. The Champion Confidence Game

1. William C. Bullitt, "How We Won the War and Lost the Peace," *Life*, Aug. 30, 1948.
2. UPI Dispatch, Dec. 2, 1961.
3. Oct. 15-16, 1962.
4. AP Dispatch, Aug. 17, 1965.
5. "In 17 Words, A Formula for Survival," p. 87 at 92, in *Peace is War*, Proceedings of the Chicago Regional Strategy Seminar, Sept. 23-24, 1960, by the Institute for American Strategy and Fifth U.S. Army Headquarters.
6. This was recommended by a Special Report of the National Strategy Committee of the American Security Council in August 1961.
7. UPI Dispatch, Oct. 30, 1964.
8. *The Communist Manifesto*, edited by Dan N. Jacobs, Row, Peterson, 1961.
9. "Cuba and Pearl Harbor: Hindsight and Foresight," *Foreign Affairs*, July 1965, p. 691.

V. Peace of the Grave

1. Dr. Gordon W. Prange, *Tora, Tora, Tora,* as published in *Reader's Digest,* Oct. 1963, p. 296.
2. *Time,* June 4, 1965, p. 13.
3. Charles Beard, *President Roosevelt and the Coming of the War,* 1941, Yale University Press, pp. 532-551; Adm. Robert A. Theobald, *The Final Secret of Pearl Harbor,* Devin Adair, 1951.
4. The Rand Corp. Translation, p. 159.
5. Senate Internal Security Subcommittee, *The Wennerstroem Spy Case,* 1964, pp. 8-9, 147-156.
6. UPI Dispatch, Mar. 26, 1965.
7. *Design for Survival,* Coward-McCann, 1965, p. 244. See *U.S. News & World Report,* Oct. 18, 1965, p. 69 for a summary of new Soviet nuclear weapons.
8. In defense of Soviet cheating on the test ban, Khrushchev said. "We would be slobbering idiots if we did not carry out the tests." *Time,* Dec. 15, 1961, p. 15.
9. *U.S. News & World Report,* Dec. 27, 1957, p. 32.
10. Speech to the Central Committee of the Communist Party of the Soviet Union, June 21, 1963, as quoted in *Peaceful Coexistence: A Communist Blueprint for Victory,* by the American Bar Association, p. 83.
11. UPI Dispatch, Moscow, Mar. 22 and 23, 1965.
12. Prof. William McGovern, former Intelligence officer for the Joint Chiefs of Staff, in speech at St. Louis YMCA, Dec. 12, 1961.
13. *Interim Report on Cuban Military Build-Up,* 1963, p. 3.
14. "Cuba and Pearl Harbor: Hindsight and Foresight," *Foreign Affairs,* July 1965, p. 701.
15. Ibid., p. 707.

VI. Eisenhower's Warning

1. Address by George F. Kennan to Women's National Democratic Club, Washington, D.C., Oct. 22, 1959.
2. Duane Thorin, *The Pugwash Movement and U.S. Arms Policy,* 1965.
3. *Bulletin of the Atomic Scientists,* April 1965, p. 9-10.
4. Senate Internal Security Subcommittee, *The Pugwash Conferences,* 1961.
5. See Chapter VIII.

6. *New York Times* News Service, July 1, 1965.
7. October 1964, p. 27.
8. "The Presidency and The Peace," April 1964, p. 353, 355.
9. AP Dispatch, Moscow, July 16, 1965.
10. *Russia and the West Under Lenin and Stalin*, p. 276.
11. Edith Kermit Roosevelt Syndicated Column, July 22, 1965.
12. ABC-TV program, July 30, 1961.
13. Senate Speech, Mar. 25, 1964.
14. *St. Louis Post-Dispatch*, June 18, 1965. The attacks on Johnson's and McNamara's policies in Vietnam and the Dominican Republic by Fulbright and other leftist Democrat Senators are a ruse, a diversionary tactic, which has created the false illusion that those policies are anti-Communist, and thereby effectively silenced justified criticism of those no-win policies.
15. Oct. 25, 1962.
16. *Study Fair*, 3 volumes, Research Papers P-3, P-6 and P-45, prepared by the Institute for Defense Analyses under U.S. Arms Control and Disarmament Agency Grant ACDA/WEC-9, June 20, 1962.
17. Speech at Arms Control Symposium, Los Angeles, Mar. 9, 1965.

VII. Six Curtains of Concealment

1. *Congressional Record*, p. 13436.
2. The *Fulbright Memorandum* devoted 15 paragraphs to an Apr. 15, 1961 speech by R. Adm. Chester Ward, USN, (Ret.), then Editor-in-Chief of the American Security Council's *Washington Report*.
3. American Security Council, *Washington Report* 61-15, Oct. 11, 1961.
4. "Free-Wheeling Disarmament Binge Endangers National Security," *Congressional Record*, July 26, 1965.
5. Feb. 5, 1965, p. 22.
6. Senate Permanent Subcommittee on Investigations, Hearings on the TFX Contract, 88th Congress.
7. Feb. 5, 1965, p. 22.
8. Senate Internal Security Subcommittee, Hearings on Otepka Case.
9. The Arms Control & Disarmament Agency paid Herman Kahn's Hudson Institute this sum (a total of $147,000) for the report entitled *Arms Control and Civil Defense*.

10. Jack Raymond, *Power at the Pentagon*, 1964.
11. Report of House Armed Services Subcommittee, 1965.
12. Rand Corp. Translation, p. 154.
13. House Appropriations Committee, Hearings on USIA Appropriations for 1966, p. 231ff., 397, 398ff.
14. Fourth Annual Report, Feb. 1, 1965, p. 25.
15. Publication 10, General Series 6, Oct. 1962.
16. American Security Council *Washington Report*, May 11, 1964.
17. *U.S. News & World Report*, June 7, 1965, p. 48.
18. *Congressional Record*, Aug. 2, 1961, p. 13437.
19. *U.S. News & World Report*, June 7, 1965, p. 48.
20. Testimony, Feb. 18, 1965, p. 45.
21. *Washington Post*, Nov. 22, 1963.

VIII. The Lie That Won the Election

1. *Newsweek*, Aug. 24, 1964, p. 21.
2. *New York Times*, Aug. 21, 1964, p. 1, 4.
3. Testimony of General John C. McConnell before House Armed Services Committee on Mar. 11, 1965, from *Hearings on Military Posture*, Feb. 2, Mar. 22, 1965, p. 1117.
4. *Saturday Evening Post*, Nov. 7, 1964, interview with McNamara.
5. *Hearings on Military Posture*, 1965, p. 211, 1118.
6. *Saturday Evening Post*, Nov. 7, 1964, p. 15; *Reader's Digest*, Feb. 1965, p. 83, *U.S. News & World Report*, Apr. 12, 1965, p. 52.
7. *U.S. News & World Report*, Apr. 12, 1965, p. 53-56; McNamara Testimony, House Armed Services Committee, Feb. 18, 1965, p. 52.
8. *Saturday Evening Post*, June 20, 1964, p. 15.
9. *U.S. News & World Report*, Mar. 1, 1965.
10. *U.S. News & World Report*, Nov. 30, 1964, p. 68.
11. Senate Preparedness Investigating Subcommittee Hearings, p. 588-589.
12. *Washington Daily News*, Apr. 14, 1964, p. 2.
13. *U.S. News & World Report*, Apr. 12, 1965, p. 52.
14. *St. Louis Post-Dispatch*, Aug. 30, 1964.
15. *St. Louis Post-Dispatch*, July 8, 1965.
16. Jan. 12, 1965; Jerome B. Wiesner, *Scientific American*, Oct. 1964, p. 28.

17. Record of UN Disarmament Commission, Apr. 26, 1965, p. 22.
18. Hanson W. Baldwin, *Foreign Affairs*, Jan. 1965, p. 265.
19. July 13, 1964, p. 11.
20. *Reader's Digest*, July 1965, p. 128. McNamara rejected the B-70 as a bomber, then later tried to cover up by saying that "a strategic version of the F-111 . . . would be sufficient to bring under attack a very large share of an aggressor's urban industrial complex." (Testimony, Feb. 18, 1965, p. 52-3.) This is completely misleading. The F-111 was designed as a Tactical Fighter — hence its original designation "TFX." General Curtis LeMay, then Air Force Chief of Staff, testified: "The main trouble with the TFX is that it is a small airplane, and it will not carry the things you need to penetrate modern defenses and still have enough range to do it. It is just not a big enough airplane to do this." (Testimony before Senate Armed Forces Committee, Feb. 19, 1964.)
21. General Thomas S. Power, *Design for Survival*, p. 161.
22. *Foreign Affairs*, Jan. 1965, p. 266-267.
23. UPI Dispatch, Moscow, July 3, 1965.
24. Dr. Stefan Possony, American Security Council, *Washington Report* 64-36, Nov. 2, 1964.
25. American Security Council, *Washington Report* 61-17, Nov. 6, 1961.
26. Speech at Los Angeles, Mar. 9, 1965.
27. McNamara Testimony, House Armed Services Committee, Feb. 18, 1965, p. 69. The comparisons are to the 1962 budget.
28. *U.S. News & World Report*, April 12, 1965, p. 59.
29. *U.S. News & World Report*, Sept. 20, 1965, p. 32.
30. *St. Louis Globe-Democrat*, July 29, 1965, p. 1.
31. *Time*, Aug. 13, 1965, p. 16; see also Interview with Chairman of Senate Armed Services Committee, *U.S. News & World Report*, Sept. 6, 1965, p. 56.
32. Aug. 16, 1965, p. 32; *National Review Bulletin*, Oct. 12, 1965, p. 4.
33. UPI Dispatch, Washington, Aug. 14, 1965.
34. William W. Kaufmann, *The McNamara Strategy*, Harper & Row, 1964; see also review of this book by Bernard Brodie, published by the Rand Corp., Mar. 1965.

35. Robert S. McNamara, "Why We Are Stronger Than Russia," *Saturday Evening Post,* Nov. 7, 1964, p. 17; *Reader's Digest,* Feb. 1965, p. 86; *Fortune,* July, 1965, p. 117.
36. *U.S. News & World Report,* Sept. 27, 1965, p. 15.

IX. Saving Face in Space

1. House Armed Services Committee, *Hearing on Military Posture,* Feb. 19, 1965, p. 379.
2. Ibid., p. 380.
3. *U.S. News & World Report,* Sept. 13, 1965, p. 36.
4. The Holmes and Hunter Alexander Syndicated Column entitled "Is Russia Outstripping U.S. in Military Space Programs?" datelined Moscow, Aug. 21, 1965, stated that "4 times in the past 2 months, *Red Star* (a newspaper published by the Defense Ministry) has trumpeted the claim that Russia now has orbital space rockets with the capacity of 'wiping any aggressor off the face of the earth' ".
5. *Newsweek,* Sept. 6, 1965, p. 46.
6. House Appropriations Subcommittee Hearings, March 12, 1964. Claims that the U.S. has the "capability" of orbital bombs or orbital rockets are completely misleading. Development of a sophisticated space payload equivalent to present Soviet actual accomplishments would require years of maximum national effort. *Future* "capability" cannot protect us against *present Soviet* orbital weapons.
7. "Russia Not Racing for Moon, Soviet Scientist Indicates," *New York Herald Tribune — Post-Dispatch* Special Dispatch, Sept. 2, 1965.
8. UPI Dispatch, Moscow, Sept. 10, 1965; There were 93 as of Oct. 19, 1965.
9. *Design for Survival,* p. 244.
10. *Time,* Sept. 16, 1965, p. 33.

X. Peace of the Knave

1. Roswell Gilpatric, *Foreign Affairs,* April 1964, p. 368; the *Fulbright Memorandum.*
2. Senators William Fulbright and Joseph Clark, *The Elite and the Electorate,* 1963.

3. Paul H. Nitze, "Power and Policy Problems in the Defense of the West," *Asilomar Proceedings,* p. 8.
4. "Foreign Policy and Christian Conscience," *Atlantic Monthly,* May 1959, p. 45.
5. *Asilomar Proceedings,* op. cit.
6. *Atlantic Monthly,* May 1959, p. 48.
7. Address to Women's National Democratic Club, Washington, D.C., Oct. 22, 1959.
8. *On Escalation,* Praeger, 1965.
9. *The Prospects for Arms Control,* ed. by James E. Dougherty with John E. Lehman, Jr., McFadden-Bartell, p. 36.
10. Speech to Convocation on *Pacem In Terris,* New York, Feb. 18, 1965
11. Oct. 1964, p. 27. 31.
12. Arthur Sylvester, Assistant Secretary of Defense for Public Information, Dec. 6, 1962.

XI. Creating the Climate

1. *An Approach to Peace,* p. 66-72.
2. *Sane World,* Apr. 15, 1964.
3. SANE pamphlet called "Mankind Must Put an End to War."
4. *Abington School District v. Schempp,* 1963, 374 U.S. 203, 227.
5. *Congressional Record,* July 25, 1953, p. 10195.
6. *Chicago Daily News.* June 22, 1964.
7. Report of the President, 1964; *The Printed Word: A Ten-Year Bibliography,* 1963.
8. P. 6.
9. *U.S.A.,* Vol. IX, No. 17-18, Aug. 24, 1962.
10. Council for a Livable World, *Washington Bulletin,* Nov. 1964.

XII. Lining Up The Liberals

1. *Witness,* p. 473.
2. *Congressional Record,* Aug. 2, 1961, p. 13437.
3. *Suicide of the West,* John Day, 1964, p. 289-290.
4. *St. Louis Post-Dispatch,* Sept. 10, 1962.

5. *Newsweek,* Oct. 9, 1961, p. 22-23.
6. *Newsweek,* June 14, 1965, p. 68.
7. Pasadena Police Department Record.
8. 13 L. ed. 2d 733, 737, Mar. 8, 1965.
9. UPI Dispatch, Berkeley, Cal., Nov. 9, 1965; material of the War Resisters League, 5 Beekman St., New York; "Draft-Dodger Schools," *New York Journal American,* Oct. 24, 1965.
10. Aug. 25, 1964, p. 17.
11. *Time,* Sept. 21, 1962, p. 17.
12. Senate Preparedness Investigating Subcommittee Hearings, Aug. 14, 1963, p. 589.
13. *Foreign Affairs,* Jan. 1965, p. 263.
14. June 14, 1965, p. 70.
15. *Wall Street Journal,* Oct. 19, 1965.

XIII Never On Sunday

1. *Russia and the West Under Lenin and Stalin,* p. 391.
2. *Saturday Evening Post,* Feb. 21, 1959, p. 10.
3. National Council of Churches, *Christian Responsibility on a Changing Planet,* p. 29-36.
4. *Sane World,* May 1965.
5. Rev. Nels F. S. Ferre, "The Church, Communism or Christ-Community," *Journal of Religious Thought,* Vol. 22, No. 1, 1965-66, p. 52.
6. Published by the Church Peace Mission, 475 Riverside Drive, N.Y. 27, N.Y.
7. Sermon entitled "No Place To Hide," Oct. 7, 1962.
8. "Catholics and Communists; Elements of a Dialogue," *A Political Affairs Pamphlet,* June 1964, p. 11.
9. "The Subversion of Pacem in Terris" by the Veritas Committee on Pacem in Terris, P. O. Box 184, Godfrey, Ill.
10. May 1965, p. 53-54.
11. *The Worker,* Oct. 10, 1965, p. 3.
12. Msgr. George G. Higgins quoted in NC Dispatch, Oct. 17, 1965.
13. *New York Times,* Oct. 24, 1965.
14. UPI Dispatch, Nov. 9, 1965.
15. *St. Louis Globe-Democrat,* Oct. 30-31, 1965, p. 1.
16. *"La Conscience du Chretien Devant L'Arme Nucleaire,"* Dec. 1964.

XIV. Partnership With the Politicians

1. Which turned out to be $4.6 billion; *New York Times,* July 15, 1965.
2. "McNamara's Management Revolution," *Fortune,* July 1965, p. 119.
3. Roswell Gilpatric, *Foreign Affairs,* April 1964, p. 370, 374.
4. *Saturday Review,* May 4, 1963, p. 10.
5. *U.S. News & World Report,* Mar. 30, 1964.
6. Feb. 8, 1965, p. 74.
7. *The New Communist Manifesto,* edited by Dan N. Jacobs, Row, Peterson and Co., p. 30.
8. House Appropriations Committee, Hearings on Department of Justice, Jan. 29, 1964, p. 305.
9. Testimony of Robert S. McNamara before the House Armed Services Committee, Feb. 18, 1965, p. 69.
10. UPI Dispatch, Mar. 2, 1965.
11. Samuel Lubell Syndicated Column, June 8, 1965.
12. Samuel Lubell Syndicated Column, June 7, 1965.
13. Statement by Senator Lyndon Johnson to the press upon convening emergency sessions of the Senate Preparedness Investigating Subcommittee, Nov. 25, 1957.
14. UPI Dispatch, Nov. 7, 1965.

XV. Peace of the Slave

1. *The Fourth Floor,* Random, 1962.
2. Senate Internal Security Subcommittee, *Communist Threat to the United States Through the Caribbean,* Part 13.

XVI. Scare-Words

1. *U.S. News & World Report,* Sept. 13, 1965, p. 58.
2. Address in Washington to labor leaders, Mar. 24, 1965.
3. *The Necessity for Choice,* Harper, 1961.
4. "New Directions in Arms Control and Disarmament," *Foreign Affairs,* July 1965, p. 587.
5. *St. Louis Post-Dispatch,* July 8, 1965.
6. Alastair Buchan, *Foreign Affairs,* July 1965, p. 584.

XVII. Striking the Profit from the Strike

1. Speech delivered in House of Representatives, July 26, 1965.
2. *U.S. News & World Report*, July 19, 1965, p. 9.
3. *Congressional Record*, Apr. 29, 1954, p. 5707.
4. "Today Asia, Tomorrow the World" by Chalmers M. Roberts, *Washington Post* Service, week of Sept. 20, 1965, carried in Honolulu *Advertiser*, Sept. 22, 1965.
5. American Security Council, *Washington Report* 65-24, June 14, 1965.
6. AP Dispatch, June 30, 1965.
7. Speech at UN, UPI Dispatch, Sept. 25, 1961.
8. How many U.S. troops have we in Vietnam, and how many more will it take to win? Background briefings given by Dean Rusk, Cyrus Vance, and other highranking Administration advisers to selected newsmen said we have 150,000 and that this figure will climb beyond 200,000. (*U.S. News & World Report*, Nov. 15, 1965, p. 44.) Carl Rowan, recent Director of USIA, wrote in his syndicated column on Oct. 31, 1965 that this figure is merely a "look-see plateau," a vantage point from which the Administration will decide how many more troops are needed. He added: "Some knowledgeable observers say that a total American commitment of 400,000 troops within a year is not unlikely."
9. Additional proof of the diversion is contained in this public message from the top Soviet theoretician Mikhail Suslov to Peking China: "One must not only speak out against them [the Western Imperialists], but *thwart their designs by concrete deeds*, applying all the wealth of tactics at the disposal of Communists." (emphasis added) (UPI Dispatch from Moscow, Oct. 5, 1965.) This official international communication by Suslov to the Chinese Reds is an urgent and clear warning of a Soviet preventive nuclear strike against the U.S. Suslov's words reek with even more hate than the *Moscow Manifesto* of 1960 and Khrushchev's speech of Jan. 6, 1961. Suslov characterizes us not merely as "aggressors," but as "atomic maniacs:" "The Communists warn the peoples of the danger of war and confidently declare that by active measures the peoples must and can thwart the aggressive plans of the atomic maniacs, curb the aggressors, tie their

hands." How can "atomic maniacs" be thwarted except by destroying them before they can destroy the world? Thus, the Suslov speech clearly reasserts and reaffirms the entire Khrushchev strategy of a preventive surprise strike against the U.S.

10. Speech in Washington, D.C., Oct. 21, 1965.

XVIII. Peace of the Brave

1. Proceedings of Asilomar National Strategy Seminar, Apr. 24-30, 1960, *Power and Law,* Chester Ward, p. 1.
2. AP Dispatch, Montreal, N.C., Aug. 16, 1965.
3. Dec. 3, 1793.
4. *Fortune,* Nov. 1965, p. 133.

ABOUT THE AUTHORS

PHYLLIS SCHLAFLY is known to millions as the author of A CHOICE NOT AN ECHO and as co-author of THE GRAVEDIGGERS, two 1964 best-sellers. Audiences from coast-to-coast know her as an eloquent advocate of the right of grass-roots Americans to determine their own future and select their own candidates without backroom control by the kingmakers or the gravediggers.

Mrs. Schlafly is an honor graduate of Washington University in St. Louis, and received a Master's Degree in Government from Radcliffe College, Cambridge, Massachusetts. She is a member of Phi Beta Kappa and of Pi Sigma Alpha, the Political Science honorary society. Her study of military affairs dates from World War II when she was a ballistics gunner and technician at the largest ammunition plant in the world.

"Phyllis Schlafly stands for everything that has made America great and for those things which will keep it that way." This is how she was described when she received the *St. Louis Globe-Democrat* Award as "Woman of Achievement in Public Affairs." She is the wife of John Fred Schlafly and the mother of six young children.

REAR ADMIRAL CHESTER WARD, U.S.N. (Ret.) was Judge Advocate General of the United States Navy, 1956-1960. He has lectured on national strategy in seminars conducted by the United States Army, the National Guard, Stanford Research Institute, the Institute for American Strategy, and the Foreign Policy Research Institute, University of Pennsylvania. He is a member of the

National Strategy Committee, American Security Council.

Chester Ward is an honor graduate of Georgetown University (B.S.) and received his LL.B. with distinction and LL.M. from George Washington University. He is a member of the Order of the Coif, and was formerly an associate professor at George Washington Law School, faculty editor of the *George Washington Law Review*, and a senior legal editor of *U.S. Law Week*. He is a co-author of the 1965 best-seller, THE GRAVEDIGGERS, and author of "The New Myths and Old Realities of Nuclear War" published in *Orbis*, Summer 1965.

Admiral Ward was awarded the Legion of Merit by President Eisenhower for his contributions to the effective use of United States seapower and his "realistic" opposition to "the Communist conspiracy."